This is a difficult time in the Church's life, yet it is also a time which God is blessing, a time rich in grace and full of hope.

—POPE PAUL VI

Catholicism & Society

Rev. Edward J. Hayes
Rev. Msgr. Paul J. Hayes
& James J. Drummey

OUR SUNDAY VISITOR, INC.

Huntington, Indiana

books in this series

CATHOLICISM AND REASON
and TEACHER'S MANUAL

CATHOLICISM AND SOCIETY
and TEACHER'S MANUAL

CATHOLICISM AND LIFE
and TEACHER'S MANUAL

Nihil Obstat:
Rev. Lawrence Gollner
Censor Librorum

Imprimatur:
✠ Leo A. Pursley, D.D.
Bishop of Fort Wayne-South Bend
July 25, 1975

ISBN: 0-87973-859-6
Library of Congress Catalog Card Number: 75-21600

Cover Design by James E. McIlrath

Second Printing, 1978

Published, printed and bound in the U.S.A. by
Our Sunday Visitor, Inc.
Noll Plaza
Huntington, Indiana 46750

859

Contents

Preface

"One loving soul sets another on fire," declared Saint Augustine. And in more recent times, Arnold Lunn, in his book *Now I See,* made this incisive and thought-provoking observation: "Christianity can sometimes be *caught* no less than taught."

This book aims to teach something of "applied Christianity" in a way that can be caught and lived.

Perhaps the underlying spirit might be expressed in the teaching of Vatican Council II in the *Decree on the Apostolate of the Laity.* "The laity must take up the renewal of the world around them as their own special obligation. Led by the light of the Gospel and the mind of the Church and motivated by Christian charity, they must act directly and in a definite way in the affairs of the world."

The book is arranged in nineteen chapters so that teachers of Christian Doctrine and group leaders may effectively utilize it for a one-year course, either for high school or adult discussion. Or the material can be utilized to provide a full-year course for Catholic high school students.

There is regular reference to The Second Vatican Council, to recent papal pronouncements, and to the Church Magisterium. Scripture quotations are from the New American Bible.

In a previous book, *Catholicism and Reason,* which is a companion book to the present volume, the authors give a popular explanation of the basic doctrines of the Catholic Faith. *Catholicism and Society* takes basic Catholic moral and dogmatic principles and *applies* them to some fundamental aspects of society in our day, such as the structure of the family, womanhood, racial justice, the aging, Marxist philosophy in today's context, and morality in public life.

Fathers Edward and Paul Hayes have been writing throughout their priestly lives. Among their books are *Three Keys to Happiness, Love for a Lifetime, Confession Aid for Children, Moral Handbook of Nursing* and *Moral Principles of Nursing,* the latter two in conjunction with Dorothy Ellen Kelly, R.N. James Drummey has written numerous magazine articles, is a teacher of high school catechetics, and is a family man with seven children.

In preparing sections of this book, the authors owe a debt of gratitude to His Eminence Humberto Cardinal Medeiros for his valuable thoughts on stewardship; to Sister Edmund and the Little Sisters of the Poor who speak from years of experience in caring for thousands of elderly, for practical thoughts on the subject; to The Christophers, whose purpose is to encourage each individual to show a personal and practical responsibility in restoring the love and truth of Christ to the market place, for their practical suggestions in the section on Communism; to Dorothy Kelly for indexing and for help in preparation of the manuscript; to James O. Kelly for his substantial help in the stewardship chapter; to Betty Thomas for typing the manuscript; and to Peter Terrafranca for doing the final reading.

One complaint of a segment of today's youth is that Christianity does not speak to the day-to-day problems of the modern man. *Catholicism and Society* seeks to do just this, at least to single out some areas where "applied Christianity" must be put into practice. G. K. Chesterton is quoted as saying: "Christianity has not been tried and found wanting. It has not been tried." This book will help to make Christianity a vital force in some areas of modern living.

Catholicism & Society

photo by Richard B. Hoffman

It is owing to his favor
that salvation is yours
through faith. This is not your
own doing, it is God's gift. . . .
You are strangers and aliens no
longer. No, you are fellow citizens
of the saints and members of the
household of God.
— Saint Paul (Eph. 2:8ff).

CHAPTER 1

The Christian Call to Action

I have come to light a fire on the earth. How I wish the blaze
were ignited! — *Luke 12:49.*
You are the salt of the earth. . . . You are the light of the
world. . . . Your light must shine before men so that they may
see goodness in your acts. — *Matthew 5:13-16*

Many Christians judge their lives on the basis of how many evils and
wrongdoings they avoided. All too few ever confront themselves with the
question of how much good they left undone.

Cardinal Reginald Pole, at the time of the opening of the Council of
Trent in 1545, challenged his fellow cardinals and the people of the world
with these words: "We are responsible for the words we ought to have said
and did not; for the things we ought to have done and did not do; for the
things we ought to have uprooted and left grow; for the things we ought to
have planted and did not plant."

The Penitential Rite at the beginning of Mass today incorporates this
same thought when we confess that we have sinned not only in thought,
word, and deed but also "in what I have failed to do."

But how many of us, at this point in the Mass, really stop to think of
the kind word that we failed to speak or the good deed that we neglected to
perform? Is there any one of us who has not walked by a new neighbor or a
new employee on the job or a new student in school without saying a
word? Who among us has not gone to a wake or a funeral and said to a
bereaved friend or relative, "Be sure and let me know if there is anything I
can do to help"? But this is little more than a gesture. The sorrowing party

is seldom able to think of something we can do and is hesitant to impose on us anyway. Instead of just talking, we could act. We could send a meal to the family or arrange to take care of the children or do any number of things that would be greatly appreciated.

Anyone who has ever been in the hospital has heard the familiar refrain afterwards, "I was sorry to hear that you were sick. I really wanted to get to visit you, but the time just got away from me." Talk like this is cheap; it is action that counts. Interestingly, excuses of this kind usually come from people who are not very busy, who have very little to occupy their time. Busy people somehow make the time to do things for other people. The old adage, "If you want something done, give it to a busy person," is still true.

The Christian layman in the world today has a solemn responsibility to God, to his church, and to his fellow man to be an instrument to "restore all things in Christ." He must begin with his own life and then this Christian spirit must overflow and permeate everything around him. The Second Vatican Council put it this way:

> The laity are called in a special way to make the Church present and operative in those places and circumstances where only through them can she become the salt of the earth. Thus every layman, by virtue of the very gifts bestowed upon him, is at the same time a witness and a living instrument of the mission of the Church herself (*Dogmatic Constitution on the Church*, No. 33).

The Council, in another of its sixteen documents, made a rather startling statement about the serious responsibility the laity have to spread the message of Christ everywhere. After noting that every member of the Mystical Body of Christ, "which is the Church," has a share in the functions as well as in the life of the body, the Council Fathers said that "so intimately are the parts linked and interrelated in this body (cf. Eph. 4:16) that the member who fails to make his proper contribution to the development of the Church must be said to be useful neither to the Church nor to himself" (*Decree on the Apostolate of the Laity*, No. 2).

THE SERMON ON THE MOUNT

The obligation of the Christian layman is clear. He is to bring the teaching and holiness of Christ to men and to influence society and its institutions in such a way as to lead all men to salvation. The blueprint for this apostolate was given to us by Christ himself in the Sermon on the Mount, particularly in the beatitudes.

When he saw the crowds he went up on the mountainside.
After he had sat down his disciples gathered around him, and he
began to teach them:

> How blest are the poor in spirit: the reign of God is theirs.
>
> Blest too are the sorrowing; they shall be consoled.
>
> Blest are the lowly; they shall inherit the land.
>
> Blest are they who hunger and thirst for holiness; they shall
> have their fill.
>
> Blest are they who show mercy; mercy shall be theirs.
>
> Blest are the single-hearted for they shall see God.
>
> Blest too the peacemakers; they shall be called sons of God.
>
> Blest are those persecuted for holiness' sake; the reign of
> God is theirs.
>
> Blest are you when they insult you and persecute you and
> utter every kind of slander against you because of me. Be glad
> and rejoice, for your reward is great in heaven; they persecuted
> the prophets before you in the very same way (Mt. 5:1-12).

Christ then indicated the impact on the world of those who live these
principles:

> You are the salt of the earth. . . . You are the light of the
> world. . . . Your light must shine before men so that they may
> see goodness in your acts and give praise to your heavenly Father
> (Mt. 5:13-16).

Saint Matthew tells us that when Jesus finished the Sermon on the
Mount, he "left the crowds spellbound at his teaching. The reason was
that he taught with authority and not like their scribes" (Mt. 7:28-29).
The scribes always quoted former rabbis, but Jesus spoke in his own name,
as one who had supreme authority: "You have heard the commandment,
'You shall not commit adultery.' *What I say to you is:* anyone who looks
lustfully at a woman has already committed adultery with her in his
thoughts" (Mt. 5:27-28). And again: "You have heard the commandment,
'You shall love your countryman but hate your enemy.' *My command to
you is:* love your enemies, pray for your persecutors" (Mt. 5:43-44).

The crowds must have also been astounded at Christ's praise for the
poor and the lowly, the merciful and the single-hearted, the peacemakers
and those who would turn the other cheek when they were insulted, persecuted, and slandered. For they lived in a land under the control of the
powerful, swaggering, and vengeful Roman Empire. The Romans were, in
the words of Saint Paul, "men without conscience, without loyalty, without affection, without pity" (Rom. 1:31).

Those listening to Jesus knew the nature of the Romans only too well.

As on other occasions, they must have found Jesus' words hard to accept. But this did not deter our Lord from speaking the hard truth. He softened the effect, however, by telling the people that "anyone who hears my words and puts them into practice is like the wise man who built his house on rock. When the rainy season set in, the torrents came and the winds blew and buffeted his house. It did not collapse; it had been solidly set on rock" (Mt. 7:24-25). The people must have been impressed with the previously unheard of principles enunciated by Jesus, for "when he came down from the mountain, great crowds followed him" (Mt. 8:1).

If the reaction of the people hearing the beatitudes for the first time seems strange to us 2,000 years later, it is only because we are familiar with them and, hopefully, have put them into practice in our own lives. However, it would not be unreasonable to say that for many people living in the last quarter of the twentieth century, the words of Christ are still hard to accept. People are too caught up in the pursuit of material and sensual pleasure to think about serving God instead of self, to reflect on the good that they are leaving undone.

It is the duty of the Catholic layman to jar these people loose from their attachment to the world and its pleasures; to remind them that a house built on sand will crumble and be destroyed; in other words, to let the light of Christ shine before men and lead them through the "narrow gate" to eternal happiness with God. Each beatitude is a beacon of light in a world darkened by sin and its effects: war, hatred, racism, immorality, greed, exploitation, indifference, persecution, and contempt for human life. The beatitudes form the basis for true Christian holiness; they must be promulgated by word and example.

BLEST ARE THE POOR IN SPIRIT

The word "blest" is an Aramaic expression of Christ that implies a sense of well-being, a true interior happiness. Those who follow these principles, Christ is saying, will be genuinely happy and their reward will be great in heaven. The word "poor" has an economic connotation in modern English. In the Bible, however, and as used by Christ, this word refers to those who are not enmeshed in the things of this world, who realize the fruitlessness of material goods, who even have become disillusioned with the world and have placed themselves completely in the hands of God. The poor in spirit are not those in abject poverty, although some may be. They are the humble of the earth; they realize their nothingness before God and their total dependence upon him. They are like little children, trusting in

God and grateful for what he is and what he does in their daily lives.

The emphasis on acquiring material goods today is nothing short of overwhelming. On radio and television, in newspapers and magazines, there is a deluge of propaganda urging us to buy the latest car or appliance or clothes, or to vacation in some exotic and faraway land. We are invited to live the "good life," to deny ourselves nothing, to eat, drink, and be merry. And yet, despite our affluence, many people are not happy. They are desperately searching for some meaning to life in the pursuit of material wealth, but the search frequently ends in disappointment, despair, and even death.

How many rich and prominent people, who appear to be sitting on top of the world, have committed suicide? The millionaire owner of the camera company was found at his desk, a suicide, with the gun still in his hand. A suicide note left on the desk said, "I have had all that life has to give. Life has no more to offer me, so I want no more life." The words of Jesus are appropriate: "Not on bread alone is man to live but on every utterance that comes from the mouth of God" (Mt. 4:4).

BLEST TOO ARE THE SORROWING

A man who converted to the Catholic Faith was asked by a friend from his wild youthful days if he was happier now that he was a Catholic. The convert replied: "If you mean, am I spiritually more happy, yes; but if you mean physically, no. Sometimes this loyalty to Christ is like walking through hell. But I would rather be walking through hell than toward it."

This story offers us some insight into the second beatitude. The sorrowing are those who remain loyal to Christ and steadfast in their faith no matter what difficulty, sadness, or tragedy may confront them. They are the ones who, in Shakespeare's words, suffer "the slings and arrows of outrageous fortune" without complaint; who grit their teeth as they struggle through school to obtain an education, or in their job to earn a living, or in their family to keep peace and harmony; who resist the temptations to neglect the worship of God, to succumb to the lure of the flesh, to cheat and steal and lie; who accept willingly the crosses that have been placed on their shoulders because they now can share in some small way in the suffering of their Savior. They are the ones to whom Christ said: "I tell you truly: you will weep and mourn while the world rejoices; you will grieve for a time, but your grief will be turned to joy" (Jn. 16:20).

Suffering and sorrow have no value in themselves; it is the reaction of the subject which can turn them to good. The spirit of resignation and union with Christ can turn adversity into virtue. Our Lord promised that the sorrowing would be consoled. How? They will have peace of mind, for one thing. A clear conscience, one that allows a person to sleep at night, is fervently desired by many people in our society. But they will not find this peace of mind until they are willing to walk through hell instead of toward it, until they can say to God, "Not my will but your will be done." The sorrowing, of course, will receive their greatest consolation in heaven, where all pain and sadness will be wiped away and they will enjoy an eternity of happiness.

BLEST ARE THE LOWLY

The word "lowly" in the Aramaic language which Christ spoke has the same meaning as "poor" in the first beatitude. The lowly or the meek are those who are submissive to God, docile to his will. They are also able to control their temper when provoked. Their refusal to do battle with everyone who crosses their path results in a generally peaceful atmosphere wherever they go.

The reward promised the lowly is the same in all the beatitudes, but in each it is presented a little differently. To inherit the land meant in the Old Testament to take possession of the Promised Land, which was the goal of Moses and the chosen people as they wandered through the desert. For Christ and his listeners it meant to obtain those things of which the Promised Land was a symbol — supernatural life and the Kingdom of God.

BLEST ARE THEY WHO HUNGER
AND THIRST FOR HOLINESS

The words "hunger" and "thirst" in the Bible signify a deep internal yearning for spiritual things. In the Old Testament, holiness was tied in with ritualistic external righteousness. Christ, on the other hand, emphasized the striving for internal goodness: "Be on guard against performing religious acts for people to see. Otherwise expect no recompense from your heavenly Father. . . . Keep your deeds of mercy secret, and your Father who sees in secret will repay you" (Mt. 6:1-4).

This beatitude also implies that it is impossible to attain interior holiness in God's sight by our own efforts alone. One does not eagerly desire that which he can have for the doing. The implication is that our daily life must be lived hand in hand with God. Then, as Christ said, we shall have our fill. The greater our hunger and thirst for holiness, the more grace God will bestow upon us.

BLEST ARE THEY WHO SHOW MERCY

This beatitude is linked with the previous one since there can be no real holiness without mercy. To be merciful means more than just showing compassion for the less fortunate and the sinful. It is the sum total of many virtues. "Because you are God's chosen ones, holy and beloved," said Saint Paul, "clothe yourselves with heartfelt mercy, with kindness, humility, meekness, and patience. Bear with one another; forgive whatever grievances you have against one another. Forgive as the Lord has forgiven you. Over all these virtues put on love, which binds the rest together and makes them perfect" (Col. 3:12-14).

Every time we say the *Our Father* we should be reminded that we must be merciful to one another: "Forgive us our trespasses as we forgive those who trespass against us." If we are merciful, Christ declared, then the mercy of God shall be ours. This promise is expressed throughout the Old and New Testament. For example, the Prophet Jeremiah tells us: "With age-old love I have loved you; so I have kept my mercy toward you" (Jer. 31:3). So too, in her canticle of praise, Mary, the Mother of God, exclaims: "God who is mighty has done great things for me, holy is his name; His mercy is from age to age on those who fear him. . . . He has upheld Israel his servant, ever mindful of his mercy" (Lk. 1:49-54).

BLEST ARE THE SINGLE-HEARTED

There is only one purpose in life: to know, love and serve God. Whatever we do — pray, play, work — must be directed to the same ultimate end. The single-hearted are those who serve God loyally for his own sake and not primarily out of self-interest. They are true and faithful to God and to neighbor. In them there is no guile or duplicity; they are honest and sincere. Single-hearted means:
conquering of ambition and pride — attachment to position
conquering of unchastity — attachment to sex
conquering of avarice — attachment to money
conquering of sensuality — attachment to the pleasure of sense.

The single-hearted shall see God, Christ promised. In this life, this means receiving gifts and favors from God and enjoying an intimate friendship with him. Possessing God through grace now will enable us to see him face to face in eternity.

BLEST TOO THE PEACEMAKERS

Two hundred years have gone by since Patrick Henry strode to the pulpit of St. John's Episcopal Church in Richmond, Virginia, and declared that "gentlemen may cry peace, peace — but there is no peace." He was referring, of course, to the imminent war with England, but his statement would be equally true today. In our own time men cry peace, peace — but there is no peace: not in the world, not in our own land, not in our communities, frequently not in our families, sometimes not even in our own hearts. The latter domain is the most important of all, for unless we have peace in our own hearts, there will not be peace anywhere else. There are no conflicts outside man that are not first waged inside him.

Peace is an essential Christian ideal and can be achieved only by living the divine principles enunciated by Christ — the Prince of Peace at whose birth the angels sang: "Glory to God in high heaven, peace on earth to those on whom his favor rests" (Lk. 2:14); the Prince of Peace who told his Apostles at the Last Supper: " 'Peace' is my farewell to you, my peace is my gift to you; I do not give it to you as the world gives peace. Do not be distressed or fearful" (Jn. 14:27).

The peacemaker is not only at peace with himself; he also prevents strife and promotes harmony in the human community. He is patient, conciliatory, and tolerant. The role of the peacemaker has been well set forth by Saint Paul: "Remain at peace with one another. We exhort you to admonish the unruly; cheer the fainthearted; support the weak; be patient toward all. See that no one returns evil to any other; always seek one another's good and, for that matter, the good of all" (1 Thes. 5:13-15).

The reward promised the peacemakers is that "they shall be called sons of God," with all the privileges that this implies. The peacemakers belong to God in a special way, they are his adopted sons and heirs: "You did not receive a spirit of slavery leading you back into fear, but a spirit of adoption through which we cry out, 'Abba!' (that is, 'Father')" (Rom. 8:15).

BLEST ARE THOSE PERSECUTED FOR HOLINESS' SAKE

This was a revolutionary idea introduced by Christ, that those who are persecuted while striving to carry out the will of God are to be considered blest. Contrast this beatitude with the previous one, which reminds the world that peace is a keynote of Christianity and that individual Christians must work for peace within themselves, between individuals, races, and nations. The paradox is that those who labor for the peace of Christ may expect persecution from the world. This should not surprise any follower of Christ, for he warned that "they will harry you as they harried me" (Jn. 15:20).

Saint Peter recognized the blessings of persecution. "Do not be surprised, beloved, that a trial by fire is occurring in your midst," he said. "It is a test for you, but it should not catch you off guard. Rejoice instead, insofar as you share Christ's sufferings. When his glory is revealed, you will rejoice exultantly. Happy are you when you are insulted for the sake of Christ, for then God's Spirit in its glory has come to rest on you" (1 Pt. 4:12-14).

Over the past twenty centuries, countless people have cheerfully given their lives rather than renounce Jesus or his Church. From the early Christian martyrs whose bodies were coated with pitch and set on fire to light the gardens of the cruel Emperor Nero, to the suffering souls undergoing persecution and death at the hands of the Communists today, we have thrilling examples of people whose reward will be great in heaven. "Whoever loses his life for my sake," Jesus promised, "will find it" (Mt. 16:25).

A BLUEPRINT FOR REFORM

The sublime wisdom and great potential of the beatitudes is admitted by many but practiced by few. "Sensible" people say that such a lifestyle is not practical; it demands too much and offers so little reward here and now. They tell us that other things are more important — power, prestige, position, pleasure. But Christ knows better. "What man thinks important," he warned, "God holds in contempt" (Lk. 16:15).

Our Lord not only taught the beatitudes, he lived them. He was poor in spirit, lowly, merciful, and suffered persecution. Yet he will not force us to keep the beatitudes. That is a choice we will have to make ourselves. Knowing our human hearts as he does, however, Christ knows that there will never be peace in those hearts, that we will never be truly happy until we follow his ideals, his way of life. Vatican II, urging "the laity to express the true spirit of the beatitudes in their lives," reaffirmed this truth:

Following Jesus who was poor, they are neither depressed by the lack of temporal goods nor puffed up by their abundance. Imitating Christ who was humble, they have no obsession for empty honors (cf. Gal. 5:26) but seek to please God rather than men, ever ready to leave all things for Christ's sake (cf. Lk. 14:26) and to suffer persecution for justice' sake (cf. Mt. 5:10). For they remember the words of the Lord, "If anyone wishes to come after me, let him deny himself, and take up his cross, and follow me" (Mt. 16:24) (*Decree on the Apostolate of the Laity,* No. 4).

A blueprint for the ethical and social reform of our modern society was given by Christ on the side of a mountain two thousand years ago. Application of this blueprint today is essential if we are to form correct attitudes toward marriage and the family, the religious life, the modern woman, the elderly, those of other races, public officials, and the Marxist-Leninists whose philosophy is diametrically opposed to that expressed in the Sermon on the Mount.

Pope Paul VI gave us our challenge:

> Let it remain for you the poor, for you the afflicted, for you who hunger for justice and peace, for all of you who suffer and weep: the Kingdom of God is for you, and it is the kingdom of happiness which comforts, compensates, gives truth to hope. Let it remain for you who have spiritually chosen Christ: he speaks in your hearts of beatitude and peace. With this ineffable gift he does not, in this life, satisfy your seeking, quench your insatiable thirst; today his happiness is only a sample, an anticipation, a token, an initiation. The fullness of life will come tomorrow, after this earthly day, but it will come, when God's own happiness will be open to those who sought him and had a foretaste of him today. God is joy!*

*General audience, December 20, 1972.

CHAPTER 2

Every Life Is a Vocation

In the design of God, every man is called upon to develop and fulfill himself, for every life is a vocation. — Pope Paul VI, *On the Development of Peoples*, March 26, 1967, No. 15

Human society with all its various stages of life is like the human body, each member of which has its own function to perform. Every member of the human body is working, each in its own way, toward a common goal — the good of the human being. Every member of human society — physician, lawyer, secretary, seamstress, truck driver, teacher, laborer, salesperson, married, unmarried — is working each in his own way toward a common goal: happiness here and hereafter.

No one, of course, no matter how seemingly lofty his vocation, should look down on the calling of another. In the words of the Vatican's *General Catechetical Directory:* "Every vocation is worthy of honor and is a call to the fullness of love, that is, to holiness; every person is endowed with his own supernatural excellence, and must be given respect" (No. 66). Or to put it in less sublime terms, consider the remark made some years ago by Oliver Nelson of Yale University Divinity School: "If all the garbage men and all the preachers quit at the same time, which would you miss first?"

God calls each of us to a particular state in life and gives each all the grace and help necessary for that state. That state is a person's vocation. In other words, your vocation is that state in life in which you can best find a measure of happiness here and secure your eternal happiness hereafter. Note the phrase, "a measure of happiness." This is important to remember because no loyal follower of Christ should expect an earthly life of uninterrupted joy and bliss. Suffering and sorrow are an integral part of life, unavoidable consequences of original sin, but they can be turned to our

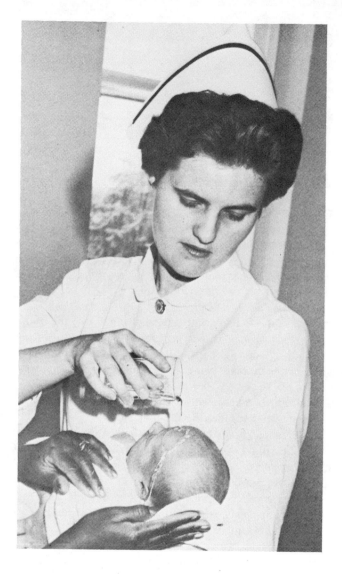

Through baptism into his death,
we were buried with him,
so that, just as Christ was raised
from the dead by the glory of the
Father we too might
live a new life.
— Saint Paul (Rom. 6:4).

eternal advantage if we understand and accept them in the spirit of the beatitudes.

Since a vocation and the conscientious fulfillment of it are very intimately connected with our eternal salvation and happiness, the question of choosing the proper state in life and of sincerely preparing for and carrying out one's vocation should be a matter of concern to young men and women and to conscientious parents. Saul of Tarsus was a zealous young man, of keen mind and willing to throw all his energies into the attainment of his ideals. Before his well-known conversion to Christianity, he gave himself wholeheartedly to the persecution of Christians. One day, while on his way to the city of Damascus, Saul was stunned by a great light from heaven and the voice of Christ. Fearful and astonished, he asked, "What is it I must do" (Acts 22:10)? Saul was told to go into Damascus where he would learn his true place in God's plan. The day of the Apostle's vocation was at hand.

God ordinarily does not work in such an unusual and miraculous fashion in calling a person to his vocation. But God, nonetheless, is calling each person to a definite state in life. "What is it I must do?" is a question that must be asked by each person who wishes to live his life according to the divine plan. The answer will not come as a bolt of light, but God does provide certain signs by which a vocation in life might be chosen. Young people especially need the help of prudent parents to find the right answer to this question. "Children should be so educated," said Vatican II, "that as adults they can, with a mature sense of responsibility, follow their vocation, including a religious one, and choose their state of life" (*Pastoral Constitution on the Church in the Modern World,* No. 52).

THE FOUR STATES IN LIFE

There are only four states in life, or vocations, in which to serve God: the single state, the religious life, the priesthood, and married life. Of course, there are many other things to be considered under each of these. A single person or one who is married may also hold a professional position or a blue-collar job. A sister or brother may devote his life to teaching, nursing the sick, social work, or missionary work. A priest may work in a parish, or teach, or work in the missions, or enter a monastery. But everyone was meant to serve God in one of the four vocations.

It is unfortunate but true today that many people seeking a vocation ask only two questions: "What do I like to do?" and "Where will I make the most money?" These are considerations, of course, but one's reasons for selecting a particular state in life must go much deeper if real happiness and fulfillment are to be found.

Everyone has a job to do in life. Cardinal John Henry Newman, the famous English Catholic convert of the last century, once said:

> God has created me to do him some definite service; he has committed some work to me which he has not committed to another. I have my mission. I may never know it in this life, but I shall be told it in the next.
>
> Therefore, I will trust him. Whatever, wherever I am, I cannot be thrown away. If I am in sickness, my sickness may serve him; in perplexity, my perplexity may serve him; if I am in sorrow, my sorrow may serve him. He does nothing in vain. He knows what he is about.

Your vocation, then, is the state in life in which God wants you to serve him in a particular way. God wants us to work with him in carrying out his divine plan so that we may be able to work toward heaven. Whatever our vocation — single, married, priest, brother, or sister — we have a mission to carry out, one that God could have accomplished himself, but for which he has chosen us as his instruments. How we perform as his chosen instruments will determine our destiny in this life and in the life to come. A brief discussion of the four states in life may help us to prepare properly for a vocation and to live it in the spirit God intended.

THE SINGLE LIFE

It never seems to occur to the average person that some men and women are unmarried because they want to be. There is no reason for us to become confused about people who stay single. Marriage is by its nature a right, not an obligation. If anyone wants to remain unmarried, all things being equal, he or she is free to do so.

We hear a great deal about vocations to the religious life, the priesthood, and married life, but let us not forget that God calls many people to the single state. Saint Paul praised those who had chosen the single life. "I should like you to be free of all worries," he said to them. "The unmarried man is busy with the Lord's affairs, concerned with pleasing the Lord; but the married man is busy with this world's demands and occupied with pleasing his wife. This means he is divided. The virgin — indeed any unmarried woman — is concerned with things of the Lord, in pursuit of holiness in body and spirit. The married woman, on the other hand, has the cares of this world to absorb her and is concerned with pleasing her husband. I am going into this with you for your own good. I have no desire to place restrictions on you, but I do want to promote what is good, what will help you to devote yourselves entirely to the Lord" (1 Cor. 7:32-35).

The majority of unmarried people who consecrate their virginity or celibacy to God are priests or brothers or sisters with public vows. But there are a number of lay people, not members of religious orders, who have made private vows of purity or virginity or chastity. Vatican II spoke highly of them in these words:

> This total continence embraced on behalf of the kingdom of heaven has always been held in particular honor by the Church as being a sign of charity and stimulus towards it, as well as a unique fountain of spiritual fertility in the world (*Dogmatic Constitution on the Church,* No. 42).

Heaven must have a special reward for the man or woman who has for some high motive chosen to remain unmarried. Many a priest in God's service owes his success to such a person. Many a gifted individual, many an outstanding pupil was formed by a patient unmarried teacher. So the next time you hear someone talk about a man or woman who "missed the boat" on marriage, point out that perhaps they are God's chosen souls, perfectly happy in their life of consecration.

No one would deny that our age demands spiritual heroism. The Church always needs consecrated single men and women, working under the guidance of priests as spiritual directors, to help in the fight against the evils of the day. If you are single, is God calling you to serve him in this special vocation?

THE RELIGIOUS LIFE

There is not a day that goes by that Christ does not invite many young men and women to go into partnership with him, to carry on his work as brothers and sisters in Catholic schools, hospitals, charitable and social agencies, and in the missions. There is so much good to be done and not enough dedicated religious to do it. Suppose a person has thought of doing this apostolic work, how can he or she recognize or judge whether a religious vocation is present? There are four factors that must be considered:

1. *Right intention and desire.* The potential candidate must want to dedicate his or her life wholeheartedly to Christ and to share in the work that brothers and sisters are doing.

2. *Physical ability.* The demands of religious life require ordinary

good health. A person need not always have been free from sickness to qualify for the religious life; normal health is sufficient.

3. *Mental ability.* The potential candidate must possess average intelligence and a willingness to study. He or she need not be the class scholar, but neither should they be below normal in class work.

4. *Moral fitness.* The interested person does not have to be a saint, or to have the spiritual qualities of a veteran brother or sister. Moral fitness means freedom from the moral ugliness of evil habits and from nasty character traits, plus a spirit of self-sacrifice, a willingness to obey, and an eagerness to please God.

If a positive response can be given to each of these points, then perhaps God is calling this young man or woman to the religious life. The next step is to discuss the matter with a priest, brother, or sister, and then to talk it over with one's parents. Parents should give guidance and encouragement all along the way, but should not interfere with the choice of a son's or daughter's vocation.

The Church in our own country would be "sorely impoverished" without the "public witness to the counsels of poverty, chastity, and obedience which religious vow, without their generous example of community life," the Catholic Bishops of the United States have told us. "The presence among us of religious is a preaching of the Gospel to the laity and the priesthood alike; in our country this preaching has been notably confirmed by the titanic work of teaching, hospital service, care of other people's children, mercy to the aged, and pioneering in social work accomplished by Catholic Sisters and Brothers who, usually anonymous and too often unthanked, have borne a professional as well as religious witness of unparalleled heroism, holiness, and achievement."*

The priest is another Christ. He alone has the merciful power to forgive sins. He alone has the miraculous power to change bread and wine into the Body and Blood of Jesus Christ. He alone, said Jean Lacordaire, the French Dominican who lived over a century ago, has a vocation "to live in the midst of the world without seeking its pleasures; to be a member of every family but belonging to none; to penetrate all secrets, share all sorrows, heal all wounds; to go from man to God and to offer him their prayers, and to return from God to man bringing pardon and hope; to have a heart of fire for charity and a heart of bronze for chastity."

*Pastoral Letter of the U.S. Bishops, *The Church in Our Day,* January 11, 1968.

It is said that the young are searching for heroes today, for people they can look up to and admire and imitate. They need look no further than the vast majority of our priests, holy and zealous men who are in the world, but not of the world; saints in the making who are doing far more good than they realize; other Christs who are always asking themselves, "What would Christ do, *now*?"

What a challenge for any young man — to be another Christ! The qualifications are the same as those for the religious life: right intention and desire, ordinary physical health, average intelligence, and moral fitness. An individual meeting these conditions should then talk over his intentions with a priest and his parents, seeking their advice and encouragement before formally making application to a seminary. An intense spiritual life, one that develops an ever-closer relationship with Christ, the Supreme and Eternal High Priest, will provide the solid foundation on which a fruitful priesthood can be built.

The Bishops of Vatican II, in addition to urging the Christian faithful to pray and work for vocations to the priesthood, also reminded them that they "should realize their obligations toward their priests and with filial love they should follow them as their shepherds and fathers. Likewise sharing their cares, they should help their priests by prayer and work to the extent possible, so that their priests can more readily overcome difficulties and be able to fulfill their duties more fruitfully" (*Decree on the Ministry and Life of Priests,* No. 9).

The same Council, wishing to assist priests in their service to the People of God, approved the restoration of the permanent diaconate as a rank in the hierarchy.

After a lapse of many centuries, the deacon is now resuming his service to the Church in the ministries of the liturgy, the word, and charity. He may administer baptism, distribute Holy Communion, witness and bless marriages, bring Viaticum to the dying, read the Gospel and preach at Mass, officiate at funerals, administer sacramentals, preside at prayer services, and help in such specialized areas as catechetics, counselling, Church administration, and public relations.

One day early in his public life, Jesus was walking along the Sea of Galilee when he saw two brothers, "Simon now known as Peter, and his brother Andrew, casting a net into the sea. They were fishermen. He said to them, 'Come after me and I will make you fishers of men.' They immediately abandoned their nets and became his followers" (Mt. 4:18-20). Jesus is still asking men to come after him two thousand years later. Let us pray that the men of today will respond to our Lord's call as quickly as Peter and Andrew did.

THE MARRIED LIFE

People have no difficulty in recognizing the priesthood or the religious life as a vocation. But how many consider marriage as a vocation? How many realize that the married state, like the other three states in life, is part of the divine plan and is a means of finding some happiness here and securing eternal happiness hereafter? Suffice it to say that far fewer marriages would end up in the courthouse and divorce if more serious thought were given to the choice of a marriage partner.

Since marriage is in the fullest sense a vocation, and is the vocation chosen by the vast majority of people, wisdom, care, and thoughtfulness must come into play when the time comes to choose a partner for life. Even a superficial knowledge of the modern-marriage situation clearly indicates that many a present-day husband or wife has not been too successful in choosing a partner. There are several reasons for this unhappy state of affairs.

First, many young people are confused by the warped theories of love promulgated through books and magazines, movies and television — theories that condone immortality and sinfulness as long as the participants allegedly love each other. This confusion prevents young people from seeking the true and solid qualities in a prospective husband or wife. Many a girl is looking for the perfect physical specimen, the "man of her dreams" with whom she can rush headlong into marriage and a life-long honeymoon. Many a boy is looking for a glamorous girl who will satisfy his sexual desires. Love becomes strictly a physical attraction and fades quickly as the physical bond deteriorates and there is no spiritual, intellectual, cultural, or emotional bond to fill the void.

Second, the modern youth seldom consults parents, priest, or a prudent adviser on such an important matter. And, many parents are reluctant to give any advice at all. Not that parents should interfere or force their will on their children, but a youth contemplating marriage may well benefit from the experience and maturity of a parent or adviser. Would a youth select a certain college or apply for a job without asking some knowledgeable person for an evaluation of the college or job?

Third, not a few young men and women enter marriage rashly, hastily, and lacking the necessary knowledge of their future spouses. The usual scenario is boy meets girl; courtship is spent almost exclusively in places of entertainment where the liquor flows freely; after a short association on this "fun and games" basis, marriage follows. The young man or woman is not marrying an individual or a personality, but rather a set of circumstances. When the circumstances change, when the "good life" is interrupted by some unforeseen crisis, a spouse may discover that the individual he or she married is not able to function very well under adverse conditions.

Fourth, many young men and women have lost sight of the very purpose of the American "dating" system and engagement period. Couples out on a date generally do not think about anything more than having a good time that evening. There is little or no thought given to the qualities one would like to see in a lifetime marriage partner. Similarly, during the engagement period, couples concentrate too much on enjoying themselves and not enough on some of the vital matters that should be discussed and agreed upon before marriage. At the very least, couples contemplating marriage ought to have reached agreement in the following areas: the purpose and sanctity of marriage, religious practice, standard of living and finances, whether the wife should work, in-laws, rights and duties of parents, outside activities, and the number of children, how they should be raised, and their religious training. Failure to settle any differences on these issues before marriage will lead to problems later on.

Fifth, many couples do not have a strong determination to make marriage work. They do not understand that marriage is an indissoluble arrangement. They hear a lot today about "trial marriages," about marriage contracts that are renewable every few years, about living together before marriage to see if a couple is compatible. The absurdity of this latter arrangement should be obvious: people who know that they can get out of a situation if the going gets tough will never try very hard to smooth over the rough spots that show up whenever two individuals try to live together as one. No marriage can be successful without a firm resolve on the part of each spouse to overlook the idiosyncrasies of the other and to overcome any difficulties with large doses of love, understanding, and patience.

"THE PERSON I MARRY"

Coming to the positive side, what are some of the qualities which a young man or woman should look for in a future spouse? What are some of the attributes which parents must know and emphasize — and exemplify in their own lives — in guiding young people preparing for marriage? What are some of the underlying factors that can contribute to a happy marriage? We can find the answers to these questions by considering four different categories: physical health, mental health, intellectual qualities, and emotional qualities.

1. *Physical health.* It is clear that a prospective husband or wife should possess moderately sound physical health. Only under extraordinary circumstances should a girl consider marriage with a man who cannot undertake the ordinary task of supporting a wife and children. Neither should she lightly link her life with one suffering from a disease which is likely to prove fatal within a few year's time. The husband as well as the wife should be free from contagious diseases, especially those of a venereal nature.

Just as the husband must be able to earn a living to support his family, so the wife must be able to discharge the duties of homemaking. She must also be able to bear and rear children without abnormal difficulty. On the other hand, minor health difficulties should not prevent a woman from having children. Modern medicine, as doctors will tell you, has solved practically all of the problems of pregnancy and childbirth.

2. *Mental health.* It is equally clear that no man or woman should marry a person who is emotionally disturbed or who is likely to become so in the near future. If marked abnormalities in emotional make-up show themselves during the courtship or engagement period, a young man or woman would do well to seek expert advice on the subject. However, a person should not regard himself as unfit for marriage simply because of insanity in some other members of the family.

3. *Intellectual qualities.* It is generally desirable that husband and wife be more or less on a par in their intellectual ability. This does not mean that college graduates should marry only college graduates. Equality of native intelligence is more important than equality of education. But if a very brilliant man or woman is matched with a dull and slow-witted partner, they will not have much true companionship and will be unable to share information and ideas about their respective careers and activities.

4. *Emotional qualities.* The number of marital problems that arise under the first three categories are miniscule compared to the marriages that have been destroyed by emotionally immature individuals. There are too many men and women who are adults in body and mental ability, but always remain children in their emotional development. They are changeable, addicted to moods and tantrums, over-sensitive, given to excessive jealousy, irresponsible, and sometimes hysterical. They make unsatisfactory husbands or wives, and are extremely unsatisfactory as

parents. As fathers and mothers, they often place children in an emotional environment which leads to delinquency, alcoholism, and mental or emotional unbalance.

It is obvious then that maturity and balance are emotional qualities to be sought in a mate. Evenness of temper, without excessive alteration of moods, is also desirable. Emotional balance should not be confused with coldness or absence of emotional response. A capacity for affection is very necessary; real coldness (as opposed to shyness) is a bad thing in a husband or wife. Warmth and heartiness, cheerfulness and enthusiasm, and a sense of humor are all pluses. But marked changes in emotions, sudden rages for reasons that would not move the ordinary person, as well as extreme jealousy and suspicion should be warning signals that an individual is emotionally unstable.

It is clear, too, that the future partner must be a good man or woman. Unselfishness is a prime quality and the major ingredient of true love — always wanting to give rather than to get, always thinking of the other person first, always wanting to make that person happy even if you do not feel like it. Honesty ranks near the top of the list, as does sincerity, understanding, patience, respect, and gentleness. Perseverance in a task and faithfulness to a promise are important. So is generosity coupled with a reasonable thrift that is free from miserliness. Modesty, in its special sense of the proper respect for sex, is an ornament both before and after the wedding day.

No person wants to marry a drunkard; no one should. People are sometimes trapped by pity into marriage with heavy drinkers; they secretly flatter themselves into believing that they will be able to change the potential alcoholic. They are like the man who built a new home on a swamp and expected that the swamp would dry up just because he built his home there. Before entering into marriage with a heavy drinker, make sure that he or she shows proof positive of reform for a long period of time.

No man or woman should marry a person of loose sexual habits under the fond belief that he or she will change after the marriage vows have been taken. It is true that God forgives and that with his grace we can reform. But before accepting a spouse with a notorious record of sexual escapades, demand positive proof of a change of ways over a period of six months to a year.

The man who is to succeed as husband and father should be truly masculine. In the dislocated society of today, we are producing a crop of masculine women and feminine men. Being masculine is not the same thing as being rough, brutal, or unfeeling. Tenderness and compassion do not conflict in any way with a really masculine temperament. The man should be vigorous, decisive, and capable of exerting leadership. He must accept the responsibility of being protector and provider to his wife and children. He should be interested in his job, proud of his workmanship, and have a reasonable desire for advancement in his chosen field. He should also accept his responsibility as a citizen in the community.

A good wife and mother should be feminine. True femininity is something quite different from fine clothes or expensive perfumes and the image of the modern woman commonly set forth in the media. Real femininity involves the qualities which go with a woman's maternal role: generosity, tenderness, sympathy, sacrifice, and total gift of self. Men should beware of girls who do not fully accept themselves as women. Far from shunning the role of motherhood, the true woman welcomes it eagerly. Like the man, the woman should be professionally competent, primarily in her homemaking tasks, but also in those outside activities which complement her role in the home. She also has a responsibility as a citizen, and housewives and mothers have had a significant impact on public issues.

If these fundamental qualities and attributes are carefully considered and put into practice, the foundation of a successful marriage will have been established. Men and women should not enter into marriage on a mere whim or superficial attraction. Their vocation should be based on common sense, prudent judgment, sound advice, and persevering prayer. Regarding the latter, a strong religious faith is absolutely essential in candidates for the married life. Every Christian marriage is a triple union — a union of two bodies, a union of two hearts, and a union of two souls. Take away any one of these and the marriage will be in trouble. Keep them intact and the married state in life will be a true vocation, bringing a measure of happiness here and leading the Christian couple to eternal happiness in heaven.

EVERY LIFE IS A VOCATION

Life can be beautiful for any man or woman who strives to serve God and to follow the teachings of Christ in one of the four vocations. Pope Paul VI gave the world an inspiring summary of the dignity of every man's vocation:

> In the design of God, every man is called upon to develop and fulfill himself, for every life is a vocation. At birth, everyone is granted, in germ, a set of aptitudes and qualities for him to bring to fruition. Their coming to maturity, which will be the

result of education received from the environment and personal efforts, will allow each man to direct himself toward the destiny intended for him by his Creator. Endowed with intelligence and freedom, he is responsible for his fulfillment as he is for his salvation. He is aided, or sometimes impeded, by those who educate him and those with whom he lives, but each one remains, whatever be these influences affecting him, the principal agent of his own success or failure. By the unaided effort of his own intelligence and his will, each man can grow in humanity, can enhance his personal worth, can become more a person (*On the Development of Peoples,* No. 15).

The family is, so to speak,
the domestic Church.
In it parents should, by their
word and example, be the first
preachers of the faith to
their children.
— Vatican Council II, *Dogmatic*
Constitution of the Church, 11.

photo by Paul J. Hayes

CHAPTER 3

The
Future of
Christian Marriage

The well-being of the individual person and of human and Christian society is intimately linked with the healthy condition of that community produced by marriage and family. — Vatican II, *Pastoral Constitution on the Church in the Modern World,* No. 47

Why should we bring up the subject of Christian marriage and family life in the context of Christianity and society today? Are not the average parents trying to live a decent life with their family, trying to earn a living, manage a home, raise children properly, enjoy a happy life, and not interfere in anybody else's problems? Besides, if there are problems in the world, in our country, in our city or town — what can we do about them? After all, every generation has said, "We hardly know what this world is coming to." Why begin raising that old cry today?

Is everything going along today just about as it always has? Or are there certain fundamental problems eating away at the very structure of family life in America — problems that must be solved?

What is happening today? And what is the future of Christian marriage and the Christian family in the closing decades of the twentieth century?

THE PICTURE TODAY

Suppose in our age of space travel a visitor from another planet were to arrive in the United States to study our family life. What would he find?

He would find the whole Christian tradition concerning the family and married life under relentless attack; contempt for human life through widespread contraception and abortion; venereal disease at epidemic levels; rampant alcoholism and drug addiction; widespread juvenile criminality; an appalling record of child abuse, and a high suicide rate among young people.

He would also find loud demands for acceptance of homosexuality and lesbianism as "alternate lifestyles"; a large number of couples living together outside of wedlock; permissive parents who have failed to instill in their children a respect for authority; a veritable flood of pornographic films and literature; and sex education programs that ignore moral teachings and promote promiscuity.

Our space traveler would discover that divorce has become socially acceptable. Cards offering "congratulations on your divorce" can be purchased in stationery stores. Gone are the long and involved legal proceedings. Many states have passed "no fault" divorce laws, which allow couples to split up without first proving that one is to blame for the break-up. There are even "do-it-yourself" divorce kits that contain all the forms needed for the handling of a divorce without a lawyer, along with instructions on filling them out.

Even Catholics cannot escape this indictment, for the divorce rate among Catholics has been just as high as the national average. The reason for this is clear: too many Catholics base their actions on the outlook, attitudes, and pressures of society, rather than the Gospel and its teachings. Archbishop Fulton J. Sheen calls them "the media people — those who will take their ideas about abortion, divorce, and morals from those that appear in the press, radio, and television."*

Some people, when confronted with these facts, will point out the other side of the coin — that most marriages do not end in divorce. But how many of these marriages are happy? How many couples are fulfilling the plan for marriage handed down by God himself? How many parents are raising their children to become responsible citizens and parents themselves? How many mothers and fathers, by word and example, are demonstrating to their children that marriage and the family offer the only real security for young people and the only real hope for the future of society?

Today there is an obvious breakdown of the influence of the Church over Catholics in general and youth in particular. Young people hear one

*"Archbishop Sheen Says Communists Confiscate Christian Principles," *The (Boston) Pilot*, March 23, 1973, p. 15.

thing in church and another at home. They are taught the virtues of purity, honesty, and truthfulness by the Church, and then come home and all too often see mother reading the latest immoral best-seller, hear father violently telling mother that birth control is none of the Church's business, read in the newspaper or watch on television as a prominent entertainer gets a fifth divorce or members of the same baseball team swap wives.

Corrupt politicians and immoral figures have had their effect on young people, especially when the proper standards and sense of values are not imparted by parents. A spirit of rebellion and lack of authority has affected the family as boys and girls do what they want and all too many parents neglect their responsibility and go along with this attitude.

The picture we have been painting, in all its revolting though factual details, shows that the institution of marriage and the family is in trouble. This does not mean, however, that the institution is obsolete or expendable. It is under stress but it can be defended and strengthened if those already married and those who will marry recognize the problem areas and work at making marriage and the family what God intended them to be. The current situation indeed offers a challenge to all thinking people — to those who still have left even a spark of love for Christian family ideals.

WHAT IS CHRISTIAN MARRIAGE?

Anyone desirous of strengthening Christian marriage must have a clear understanding of the divine origin and sacramental nature of marriage. We can easily arrive at such an understanding by consulting four major Church documents — Pope Pius XI's landmark encyclical on Christian marriage, *Casti Connubii* (1930); the Second Vatican Council's *Pastoral Constitution on the Church in the Modern World* (1965); Pope Paul's prophetic encyclical on the regulation of birth, *Humanae Vitae* (1968), and the pastoral letter of the United States Catholic Bishops, *Human Life in Our Day* (1968).

The same theme runs through all of these documents: marriage owes its existence to God, and its origin dates from the very beginning of mankind; Christ later elevated the state of marriage to a sacrament through which Christian spouses receive the grace to fulfill their marital and family obligations and lead each other to God; the Christian family is the foundation of society and manifests to all men the presence of Christ in the world.

In the earliest pages of the Bible, we find God instituting marriage by bringing the first man and woman into existence and telling them to "be fertile and multiply; fill the earth and subdue it" (Gn. 1:28). Many centuries later, the Son of God came on earth and confirmed his Father's plan: "At the beginning of creation God made them male and female; for this reason a man shall leave his father and mother and the two shall become as one. They are no longer two but one flesh. Therefore let no man separate what God has joined" (Mk. 10:5-9).

Jesus also showed us his respect for the institution of marriage when, at the beginning of his public life, he attended the wedding feast at Cana. Our Lord, whose three years of public life were so crowded, took time to be present at Cana not only for the sake of recreation and sociability, but even more to give his stamp of approval, to consecrate and elevate matrimony by his presence.

Still further evidence of Jesus' high regard for marriage is his reply to the question about why his disciples did not fast. "How can wedding guests go in mourning so long as the groom is with them?" he asked. "When the day comes that the groom is taken away, then they will fast" (Mt. 9:15). Christ found it altogether appropriate to compare himself to the bridegroom and his disciples to the guests at a marriage feast.

What God the Father ordained, and Jesus upheld, Saint Paul taught. The Apostle saw the intimate love between a husband and his wife as symbolic of the love between Christ and his Church. He said that a wife should submit to her husband as the Church submits to Christ, and that a husband should love and care for his wife as Christ loves and cares for his Church. Calling attention to the passage from Genesis about a man leaving his parents and clinging to his wife, Saint Paul said that "this is a great foreshadowing; I mean that it refers to Christ and the church" (Eph. 5:32).

What Saint Paul taught two thousand years ago, his namesake, Pope Paul VI, taught in our day. Marriage, the Holy Father has said, "is the wise institution of the Creator to realize in mankind his design of love. By means of the reciprocal personal gift of self, proper and exclusive to them, husband and wife tend towards the communion of their beings in view of mutual personal perfection, to collaborate with God in the generation and education of new lives. For baptized persons, moreover, marriage invests the dignity of a sacramental sign of grace, inasmuch as it represents the union of Christ and of the Church" (*Humanae Vitae*, No. 8).

Marriage, then, even as a human contract, has a divine dignity by reason of its very nature, by reason of its origin from God, and by reason of Christ's elevation of it to one of the seven sacraments. That is the difference between marriage and matrimony. Matrimony confers grace — a sharing in the life and love of God — upon baptized persons who enter this state.

The sacrament of matrimony was instituted by Christ as an outward sign both of God's grace and man's faith. When the bride and groom administer this sacrament to each other, they begin sharing together in Christ's grace. They will have this supernatural assistance for all the years of their married life, to help them overcome difficulties or disappointments, to cope with every situation. The bishops of Vatican II summed up the significance of matrimony this way:

> Christian spouses have a special sacrament by which they are fortified and receive a kind of consecration in the duties and dignity of their state. By virtue of this sacrament, as spouses fulfill their conjugal and family obligations, they are penetrated with the spirit of Christ. This spirit suffuses their whole lives with faith, hope, and charity. Thus they increasingly advance their own perfection, as well as their mutual sanctification, and hence contribute jointly to the glory of God (*Pastoral Constitution on the Church in the Modern World*, No. 48).

THE TWOFOLD PURPOSE OF MARRIAGE

Happiness in marriage depends on your philosophy of marriage, on what you think marriage is all about, on what you see as the purpose of marriage. The secular society in which we live says that the purpose of marriage is pleasure — what can I get out of it? In their selfish pursuit of pleasure for its own sake, the secularists condone and encourage a wide variety of immoral actions — contraception, sterilization, abortion, adultery, and finally, if none of these aberrations can guarantee maximum carnal pleasure, there is always divorce. The results of this false outlook on marriage are painfully apparent today.

The Catholic Church, on the other hand, faithful to the teachings of its Founder, presents a philosophy of marriage that views the married state as a symbol of the union between Christ and his Church and an opportunity for the couple to attain happiness and holiness in this life and in eternity. Marriage, the Church teaches, has a twofold purpose: (1) the procreation and education of children, and (2) the development of mutual love and sanctity between husband and wife. If either purpose is compromised, the marriage and the family will suffer. The two aspects of marriage are inseparable.

The same can be said of the marital act itself. Marital intercourse has a twofold meaning — life-giving and love-giving — and it is a mutilation of the act to deprive it of either meaning. A person who forces sexual acts on a spouse against his or her reasonable wishes deprives the act of its love-giving aspect. So, too, spouses who practice contraception deprive the act of its life-giving meaning. The two purposes of the sexual act were designed by God the Creator. To disregard either one is to contradict not only the nature of both man and woman and their most intimate relationship, but also the plan of God and his divine will.

Pope Paul, in a beautiful defense of life and love, declared that man on his own initiative cannot break "the inseparable connection . . . between the two meanings of the conjugal act: the unitive meaning and the procreative meaning. . . . By safeguarding both these essential aspects, the unitive and the procreative, the conjugal act preserves in its fullness the sense of true mutual love and its ordination towards man's most high calling to parenthood" (*Humanae Vitae*, No. 12).

The correct philosophy of marriage can be illustrated by drawing a large triangle. Put the word "husband" in the left corner and the word "wife" in the right corner. Put the word "God" at the top and the word "children" in the center of the triangle. There is the true Christian philosophy of marriage — a partnership in sanctity, a union with God.

Never forget that triangle. No matter what you hear the "media people" say, that triangle is the only true philosophy of marriage, and consequently the only one upon which a man and woman can build their happiness. Any Christian marriage that falls short of this ideal will flounder helplessly. When these fundamental components of marriage are rejected, then family life, the individual, and the nation suffer. There cannot be a violation of God's moral norms, of his divine plan, without repercussions. And when God's laws are rejected on a wide scale, the nation suffers.

THE PLAGUE OF DIVORCE

In an age of widespread licentiousness and rejection of traditional moral values, the Catholic Church's prohibition of divorce must seem old-fashioned and foolish. To couples with seemingly insurmountable marital problems, this prohibition must seem particularly harsh and lacking in compassion. Does the Church have to be so strict? Is it not time for the Church to re-evaluate its position on divorce and remarriage?

The simple answer to all of these questions is the same: the Catholic Church cannot allow divorce because Jesus Christ ruled it out. The Catholic Church prohibits divorce because Christ himself prohibited it. Jesus knew well the devastating effect that divorce would have on family life and society, and so he spoke repeatedly and clearly on the nature of marriage and the question of divorce.

Our Lord's teaching on divorce can be found in two places: in the Sermon on the Mount and on the occasion when a group of Pharisees asked him a question to test his credibility. In the first instance, Jesus, comparing the teaching of the old law and the prophets with his own teaching, said: "It was also said, 'Whenever a man divorces his wife, he must give her a decree of divorce.' What I say to you is: everyone who divorces his wife — lewd conduct is a separate case — forces her to commit adultery. The man who marries a divorced woman likewise commits adultery" (Mt. 5:31-32).

The apparent exception for lewd conduct has puzzled people for centuries. Biblical scholars are not agreed on the meaning of the phrase. That Jesus was not sanctioning divorce for any reason, however, is clear from his other statements, and from the teaching of Saint Paul, the teaching of the early Church, and the consistent reaffirmation of his prohibition by his Church down to our own century.

The incident involving the Pharisees gave Jesus another opportunity to state his position on divorce. The Pharisees, trying to trip Jesus up, asked him whether it was permissible for a husband to divorce his wife. Our Lord replied that when a man and woman marry, "they are no longer two but one flesh. Therefore let no man separate what God has joined" (Mk. 10:8-9). Later, when his disciples began to question him about this, Jesus told them: "Whoever divorces his wife and marries another commits adultery against her; and the woman who divorces her husband and marries another commits adultery" (Mk. 10:11-12).

Saint Paul, in his preaching, reiterated Christ's prohibition of divorce and emphasized that it was our Lord's prohibition and not his own: "To those now married, however, I give this command (though it is not mine; it is the Lord's): a wife must not separate from her husband. If she does separate, she must either remain single or become reconciled to him again. Similarly, a husband must not divorce his wife" (1 Cor. 7:10-11).

Twenty centuries later, the Second Vatican Council labeled divorce a "plague" and a profanation of the sacrament of matrimony (*Pastoral Constitution on the Church in the Modern World,* Nos. 47, 49). And on May 15, 1974, shortly after the people of Italy had voted against repeal of the country's divorce law, Pope Paul told an audience of newly-remarried couples that the basic properties of marriage are "indissolubility and faithfulness" and that "the law of God and of the Church" regarding divorce "has not changed."

Jesus' strict teaching on divorce, like all of his teachings, makes good sense in the practical order. The very nature of marriage and the family demands an indissoluble bond. The good of both husband and wife and of the children must stand or fall with the marriage tie. What would become of children if parents could separate at their own pleasure? A look today at the homes of divorced parents, and the consequences for the children involved, proves the need of marriage for life. Divorce has brought with it far more hardships and much more unhappiness in the world than marriage fidelity with its trials and sacrifices. Experience and observation will show that by and large the most unhappy and discontented people in the world are not those who are married to one partner for life, but those who have been divorced one or more times.

There are many reasons why married couples seek divorces: lack of true love, sexual immaturity, marital infidelity, false ideas and practices of responsible parenthood, lack of money, drinking, and so forth. Most of these excuses could be listed under the first one, lack of true love, or, in one word — selfishness. None of these problems are insurmountable. Their solution can be found by studying any successful marriage with its qualities of large-heartedness and forgiveness and true spiritual love — a benevolent love that consists of giving and sacrificing, of always being solicitous for the happiness and salvation of the spouse.

Every law made for the general welfare may mean some hardship in a particular case. Quarantine laws, for instance, frequently impose inconvenience on individuals, but we do not for that reason abolish the laws. Similarly, the Church cannot change its divorce laws just because certain hardship cases exist — and they do exist. The only thing that the Catholic Church can do in such extreme situations is to allow the husband and wife to separate but not of course to remarry.

At the same time, the Church, through its priests and religious, the laity, and its agencies, shows compassion and concern for the victims of broken marriages. There is a great need for understanding and assistance for men and women who suddenly find themselves alone in a new lifestyle with no companionship, few friends, little money, new responsibilities, and a sense of loneliness and even despair.

What divorcees or separated people want most at a time like this is acceptance by others, to be treated with respect and dignity and not scorned as a pariah. They also need competent and sympathetic help, financial aid, moral support, and spiritual guidance to remain faithful to their Catholic religion. (Bear in mind that it is not divorce but remarriage that separates a Catholic from his Church.) Positive efforts are being made today to cushion the traumatic effects of a broken marriage; they deserve support and participation.*

WHAT OF THE FUTURE?

There are serious problems facing Christian marriage today. One could try to ignore these problems, or to wish them away, or to despair of ever solving them. But this is not the Christian way. As in so many other areas of our society, the Christian is called to action. He is called first to put his own spiritual and moral house in order, and then to permeate society with Christian principles and example.

Christian marriage will survive this and future ages if married couples understand, promulgate, and live the true philosophy of Christian marriage; if they meet the problems head on and work within their own families and with other families to solve them; if they demonstrate that Christian marriage is vitally important for the spiritual and social well-being of the couples themselves, their families, and society in general. Pope Paul gave Christian husbands and wives their charge:

Christian married couples . . . must remember that their Christian vocation, which began at baptism, is further specified and reinforced by the sacrament of matrimony. By it husband and wife are strengthened and as it were consecrated for the faithful accomplishment of their proper duties, for the carrying out of their proper vocation even to perfection, and the Christian witness which is proper to them before the whole world (*Humanae Vitae*, No. 25).

*William J. Nessel, O.S.F.S., "The Catholic Divorcee — a Pastoral Approach," *Homiletic & Pastoral Review*, March, 1973, pp. 10-16.

Happy the husband of a good wife,
twice-lengthened are his days;
a worthy wife brings joy
to her husband,
peaceful and full is his life.
— (Sir. 26:1-2).

CHAPTER 4

Between Husband and Wife

Marriage to be sure is not instituted solely for procreation. Rather, its very nature as an unbreakable compact between persons, and the welfare of the children, both demand that the mutual love of the spouses, too, be embodied in a rightly ordered manner, that it grow and ripen. — Vatican II, *Pastoral Constitution on the Church in the Modern World,* No. 50

At times the discussion of the subject of marriage and the family is so concerned with the modern evils of divorce, artificial birth control, and neglect of parental duties, that we are apt to get an unbalanced picture. There is a danger today even among good people that a negative instead of a positive attitude may be built up. Certainly we must avoid the moral diseases and errors prevalent today. But we must do more — we must look at the positive side and build up a strong, healthy, revitalized family. The first step in this process involves a discussion of the proper relationship between husband and wife.

Marriage is a sacred vocation. It is the state in life to which husbands and wives have been called by God from all eternity. Their meeting, attraction to each other, and decision to set up a Christian home are not the result of blind chance, but are part of the Creator's divine plan. As instruments of God, husbands and wives are involved in a holy and noble undertaking. They have a responsibility not only for their own salvation, but also that of their spouses and their children. How important it is then that husbands and wives understand the earthly and heavenly ramifications of their state in life, and work unceasingly to mold their marriages into the supernatural unions that God wants them to be.

THREE PILLARS OF MARRIAGE

Where do we begin? How does a couple go about building a happy and holy marriage? Are there certain basic foundations upon which a successful marriage can be constructed? People who have studied marriage and marriage problems are generally agreed on the importance of three foundation stones or pillars that should undergird all marriages: information, communication, and application.

Information. If there is one subject about which there is voluminous information, it is the subject of marriage. From every corner of the printed and electronic media we are deluged with suggestions on how to improve your marriage. Much of this material is worthless junk. No normal husband or wife would ever have the time to go through all of this information, and to sort out the good from the bad. So where do conscientious spouses look for sound information on marriage?

One obvious source, to which we have already referred a number of times, is the Bible, particularly the New Testament. Much valuable and thoroughly reliable information on marriage, and all phases of life, can be found in the Gospels and the letters of Saint Paul. A related source of solid information is the teaching authority of the Catholic Church, that is, the writings, addresses, and deliberations of the popes and the bishops. Such documents as Vatican II's *Pastoral Constitution on the Church in the Modern World,* Nos. 47-52; Pope Paul VI's encyclical letter, *Humanae Vitae,* and the U.S. Catholic Bishops' pastoral letter, *Human Life in Our Day,* are of great value to couples seeking the Church's attitude towards married life and the family. Books and manuals written by people with a sensible and Christian outlook on marriage are also sources of helpful information.*

Finally, married couples can learn by observing other married couples, especially those who appear to have attained a happy and holy marriage. Such lucky couples are more numerous than you think. They might be in your own family, or next door. You have already noticed them, the way they talk to each other, the joy they experience in doing things together, the way their children reflect credit on them. There is an unmistakable aura of love and happiness about them. They are not perfect; once in a while, you catch them acting very humanly. But for the most part, they are

---

*For instance: *The Freedom of Sexual Love* and *Marriage Is for Grownups* by Joseph and Lois Bird; *Love in Marriage* by Henri Gibert, M.D.; *Between Husband and Wife* by Victor Salz, and *The Sexual Marriage* by Edward P. Sheridan and Kathleen Sheridan.

in complete control of their situation and offer a shining example of a true matrimonial partnership with God.

Communication. Marriage counselors are agreed that the vast majority of problems between spouses can be traced to poor communication between them. One survey concluded that 87% of all marital problems originate in the failure of husbands and wives to communicate adequately with each other. The following complaints are typical: "My wife doesn't understand me." "My husband won't talk to me." "We can't carry on a civil discussion, we always wind up fighting." "We seldom talk to each other anymore."

By communication we do not mean conversation. Many couples have no difficulty talking to each other, but they do not communicate. They discuss all kinds of trivial matters in order to avoid the major problems that are really troubling them. Other couples do communicate — verbally, with facial expressions or gestures — but they never reach a mutual understanding of each other or their problems. They argue or shout or give each other the silent treatment. Instead of listening to what their partner is trying to say, they are busy thinking of a retort that will put their spouse in his or her place.

What then do we mean by communication? *We mean a constructive and open attempt to reach a mutual understanding and knowledge of each other.* The main consideration in this process, as in all aspects of married life, must be the thoughts, feelings, and reactions of the other person. True communication exists when both spouses are sincerely interested in what the other partner thinks. And when there is disagreement, they discuss their differences calmly and lovingly. There are no harsh or unkind words; there is no ridicule; one partner does not say to the other, "How can you be so stupid as to think such a thing?" Putting it at its simplest: Couples should treat each other as they would like to be treated.

The only way that a man and woman can really get to know each other and to grow in love is to talk openly and constructively about the things that are most important to them — love and sex, God and children, money and work, relatives and friends, politics and play. On most things couples will agree. When they do not, each will have to give a little, or perhaps a lot. This giving should not be done grudgingly or resentfully, but generously. It will not be easy; it could be very painful. Couples who truly love each other, however, will make the sacrifice, and will unselfishly put their spouse's feelings ahead of their own. The result will be a peaceful and happy marriage.

There are a few basic principles to keep in mind:

1. *Always bring grievances into the open.* If a husband is annoyed because his wife's family comes to dinner every Sunday, or a wife is angry because her husband never calls when he has to work late, they should discuss the difficulty openly with each other. Ignoring the problem will not make it go away. It will only fester and may break out later in a violent manner. Bring the grievance out in the open where it can be discussed and resolved.

2. *Do not magnify minor irritations.* All of us are confronted with petty annoyances every day. They are not worth getting excited about and should be overlooked, or handled in a low-key manner.

3. *Always make the meaning of your words clear.* Just as debaters should define their terms, so couples interested in improving their communication should make sure that they are not being misinterpreted or misunderstood. Never assume that your partner knows what you are talking about. An amazing number of marital problems could be avoided if spouses were clear and precise in their communication. In the same vein, spouses should never attempt to read more into a remark than was intended. "I heard what you said," says one mate, "but I *know* what you *really* meant." Try not to be like the two psychiatrists who said, "Good morning," as they passed on the street and then walked away thinking, "I wonder what he meant by that."

4. *Avoid angry words and bitter statements.* Guard against harsh and cutting words that you will regret later. No matter how many kind words may be spoken in the months and years after a shouting match, somehow we never forget the nasty remarks. Spouses who find themselves on the verge of losing their temper should say a prayer for patience or, as a last resort, take a walk. There is a story about an eighty-year-old man who went to the doctor for a check-up and was found to be in excellent health. Asked for an explanation, the old man replied: "When my wife and I were married, we made a promise that whenever she got angry, she would leave the room and do her housework elsewhere. Whenever I got angry, I would leave the house and take a long walk. And, Doc, for sixty years I've had the greatest outdoor life you ever did see."

5. *Never let bitterness carry over until the next day.* Even if you cannot agree on a problem, grant your partner's sincerity, exchange a good night kiss, and resolve to resume the discussion on a friendly basis the next day.

6. *Keep disagreements between yourselves.* Nothing will destroy communication between husband and wife faster than involving relatives, friends, or neighbors in disagreements. What mate would speak freely again after having confidential statements carried to outsiders? There is one exception to this rule: if serious problems continue unresolved over a long period of time, endangering the stability of the marriage, then a qualified advisor, such as a priest or a trained marriage counselor should be consulted.

Application. Once married couples have acquainted themselves with sound information, and have established constructive lines of communication, the other requirement necessary for a successful marriage is application, not just when troubles arise, but every single day. It is usually small and seemingly unimportant things, such as daily displays of moodiness, lack of consideration, disinterest in a partner's activities, that lead to the deterioration of a marriage, not major crises or disasters. Hence, a happy relationship demands day-by-day evidence of cheerfulness, concern for a spouse's feelings, and genuine interest in the husband's job or the wife's home-making routine. One of the worst things a couple can do is to take each other for granted. Little things do mean a lot. Frequent compliments and indications that you care will go further than huge displays of generosity and attention only on a birthday or an anniversary.

We all can whip up enthusiasm for a major event now and then. The hard part is concentrating on the small details without which the major event would be a failure. The same is true of marriage. Getting excited about a birthday party or an anniversary celebration is comparatively easy; devoting attention to the minor matters that influence the success or failure of a marriage the other 363 days of the year is difficult. Couples who value a joyful and fruitful marriage will not neglect this vital matter.

FIVE BASIC QUALITIES

There was a popular song many years ago, one verse of which went like this:
Will someone kindly tell me,
Will someone let me know,
Why I picked a lemon in the garden of love,
Where they say only peaches grow!

That song, in a humorous way, reflects what is happening all too often today when we consider the skyrocketing divorce rate in the United States. Of course, the question of matrimonial peaches or lemons is at times relative. A person who is a peach to one may be a lemon to another. But there are certain characteristics which, when present, will make a "peach" of a husband or wife, mother or father. In a Christian sense, we might consider five such basic qualities — chastity, unselfishness, affection, sexual love, and humility.

Chastity. If the Christian ideal of chastity *before* marriage strikes many in our sex-saturated society as old-fashioned and repressive, they must be incredulous at the thought of chastity *within* marriage. "Are you kidding?" one can hear them say. "Anything goes in marriage. There are no restrictions." The plain fact is, however, that chastity is an essential requirement for a happy and holy marriage.

Couples who enter the married state with visions of unlimited sexual pleasure are in for a big surprise. Like any other bodily appetite, sex can be abused and must be curbed at times for the physical, social, and spiritual well-being of the spouses. For instance, during times of illness, or unavoidable separations, or before and after the birth of a child, couples must practice continence, that is, they must abstain from sexual relations. For unselfish spouses, these temporary situations will pose no serious problems.

There will also be cases where the wife may be unable to bear children without grievous risk to her health or even to her life, or where couples may be financially unable to support another child, or where there may be other serious reasons for spacing out births. Under these conditions, there are only two possible solutions: the moral practice of continence or the immoral practice of contraception. The choice Catholic couples make will depend on several factors: their spiritual life, their responsiveness to the teachings of their Church, and their strength of character.

If couples have never practiced any Christian self-denial, if God has no place in their married life, if they consider the teaching of the Holy Father as just one of many options, if they accept the view of the "media people" that sexual gratification is the ultimate goal of a man-woman relationship, then continence will seem like an impossible, unreasonable, and even detrimental practice. Again, however, the facts are at variance with the prevailing attitude in our modern society, as thousands of happily married couples can testify.

Continence is not only possible, it is desirable in married life. With the mutual consent and affirmative support of both partners, it can enhance the enjoyment of the marital act and raise it from a purely mechanical function to a deeply spiritual union. Furthermore, continence is an absolute requirement for Christian living, offering an alternative to such illicit practices as contraception and adultery.

It must be conceded, however, that continence, in and of itself, is a negative concept. Viewed strictly in this light, it is not difficult to understand why it would seem repressive and out of reach by those who live in spiritual mediocrity, who are obsessed with a hedonistic philosophy of life, who are governed by selfishness rather than by love. But this is not the case when continence is linked with the positive virtue of chastity. In marriage chastity means the integration of sexual love with the procreative end of marriage, as God intended, instead of selfishly seeking sexual pleasure as an end in itself.

It is much easier to make such a statement than it is to live up to it. No one in his right mind would ever suggest that the practice of continence and chastity in marriage is not a terrific struggle. But to couples with strong convictions about life and love, who seek the help of God through constant prayer and frequent reception of the sacraments of penance and the Holy Eucharist, the ideal of chastity will become, if not easy, at least attainable.

The discipline of chastity, "far from harming conjugal love, rather confers on it a higher human value," Pope Paul said. "It demands continual effort, yet thanks to its beneficent influence, husband and wife fully develop their personalities, being enriched with spiritual values. Such discipline bestows upon family life fruits of serenity and peace, and facilitates the solution of other problems; it favors attention for one's partner, helps both parties to drive out selfishness, the enemy of true love, and deepens their sense of responsibility" (*Humanae Vitae*, No. 21).

Unselfishness. Of all the traits necessary in family life, wholehearted unselfishness has to rank near the top of the list. There can be no successful family life without it. The good of one's partner and the common good of the family must come first, and that means generosity and at times self-sacrifice. Anyone who is really earnest about his marriage and family will put his own wishes and desires in second place rather than first. An excellent illustration of this quality can be found in the short story, "The Gift of the Magi," written by the famous author, O. Henry.

A young man and wife living in one of the poorer sections of New York were struggling to get along financially. Della had one thing she prized very much, her beautiful hair; Jim was very attached to one of his few earthly possessions, a pocket watch. These things were very dear to them — little things, perhaps, but they meant a lot to them. It was Christmas Eve and Della had only a few dollars to get a present for Jim. Jim had a meager income and had little left to get a present for Della. While he was at work, Della went to a beauty parlor and sold her hair. With the money she bought a beautiful watch chain that Jim had wanted for some time. Jim came home on Christmas Eve and was dumbfounded when he saw Della's hair. He handed her a package. It contained an expensive set of combs which he had bought with the money he obtained by selling his watch. Della then gave Jim the watch chain.

The point of the story is that both were willing to give up their most precious possession for the sake of the other. This principle is also summed up well in the instruction that for many years was given to couples before marriage:

It is most fitting that you rest the security of your wedded life upon the great principle of self-sacrifice. . . . Henceforth you belong entirely to each other; you will be one in mind, one in heart, and one in affections. And whatever sacrifices you may hereafter be required to make to preserve this common life, always make them generously. Sacrifice is usually difficult and irksome. Only love can make it easy; and perfect love can make it a joy. We are willing to give in proportion as we love. And when love is perfect, the sacrifice is complete.

Affection.   According to the dictionary, affection means love, a word very much misunderstood today. Ask ten people to define love and you will probably get ten different answers. Someone has put it this way: "Love is a certain force within a person leading him to lay all he is and all he has at the feet of the one he loves." And that is a good test of love. It is not so much measured by sentiment, physical attraction, or mere words, but by how much you are willing to give, how much you are willing to sacrifice for the one you love. The true Christian family must be based on this solid love expressed by deeds. Never once in the Gospels is Mary reported as saying to her Son, "I love you." Her love was obvious from the way she acted. Thus the important thing is not so much what is said, but what is done, what is sacrificed willingly.

Saint Paul, himself unmarried, gave a summary of love that married couples would do well to take to heart: "Love is patient, love is kind. Love is not jealous, it does not put on airs, it is not snobbish. Love is never rude, it is not self-seeking, it is not prone to anger; neither does it brood over injuries. Love does not rejoice in what is wrong but rejoices with the truth. There is no limit to love's forbearance, to its trust, its hope, its power to endure" (1 Cor. 13:4-7).

Affection in marriage can be expressed in countless ways. There are physical expressions, such as spontaneous kisses and thoughtful actions; intellectual expressions, such as constructive discussions of all matters which affect husband, wife, and family; and spiritual expressions, such as praying together and living together in the way that God intended.

Sexual love.   One of the great ironies in our sex-saturated society is that so many people are so woefully ignorant about the facts of life and love. Hence the popularity of sex manuals and of men and women who claim to be "experts" in this field. The availability of this information, however, has not diminished the number of people who are confused about their sexuality, primarily because the material is concerned almost exclusively with the physical aspects of sex and hardly at all with its spiritual dimensions.

Sexual intercourse in marriage is a sacred act that was designed by God to provide mutual pleasure to a husband and wife and at times a new life. There is no other way to bring children into the world. In the words of Vatican II: "The actions within marriage by which a couple are united intimately and chastely are noble and worthy ones" (*Pastoral Constitution on the Church in the Modern World*, No. 49).

Husbands and wives must treat each other as persons, not things. They must be gentle, patient, considerate, and sensitive to each other's feelings. Love-making without mutual affection and tenderness is nothing more than having sex. Love must be more than just the marital act itself; it must be a morning, noon, and night endeavor by both spouses that includes frequent signs of affection and concern.

If there is true love, understanding, tenderness, patience, and spiritual and emotional rapport between a husband and wife, their relationship will nearly always result in pleasure and joy. Married couples should occasionally reexamine their own attitudes toward love. They should honestly discuss their needs and difficulties with each other and work to improve their relationship if it needs improving. If they are unable to resolve problems, they should consult a qualified and skilled marriage counselor.

Humility.   The late Cardinal James Gibbons once said: "If we examine the sources of our troubles and agitations, we find that they almost invariably spring from a desire of appreciation or a fear of contempt." Witness the reaction of the wife whose husband has forgotten to bring home flowers for her birthday. "You don't love me any more!" she says. Or the husband whose toast is burned says, "I guess the honeymoon is over!" Many a family difficulty could be averted, many a heartache done away with if humility were put into practice.

Humility does not mean becoming a "shrinking violet" or walking around the house with your head down, telling all who listen how wrong you are. Humility is truth; it is realizing that we have good qualities and bad qualities, and that the good is from God and the bad from us. If humility of this kind is practiced in the home, then God becomes a part of family life. And what better model of humility could we look up to than our blessed Lord, "who humbled himself to share in our humanity?" The Son of God became man, was born in a stable when he could have been born in a palace, and died as a criminal on a cross. What more evidence do we need that humility must be a part of our life?

It takes a humble person to admit his error, to give in when he is wrong, to put up with life's small, constant difficulties and annoyances. How many marriages would improve tomorrow if both spouses swallowed their pride and resolved to introduce some humility into their lives? It was to those who can overlook the minor faults of others because they are so very aware of their own faults that Christ said, "Blest are the lowly; they shall inherit the land" (Mt. 5:5).

SOME IMPORTANT DIFFERENCES

The success or failure of the lifelong partnership of marriage depends on many factors. Holding an important place among those factors, as we have seen, is mutual understanding. It is precisely here that so many couples fail. They do not understand the important differences between men and women. As a result, husbands try to fit wives into a masculine pattern, and wives look at husbands from the feminine viewpoint. This is a mistake because men differ from women in many ways — in their respective vocations, their intellectual processes, and their emotional natures. A mutual understanding of these differences will go a long way towards guaranteeing a happy marriage.

Respective vocations. Nearly two thousand years ago, Saint Paul summed up the roles of Christian wives and husbands:

Wives should be submissive to their husbands as if to the Lord because the husband is head of his wife just as Christ is head of his body the church, as well as its savior. As the church submits to Christ, so wives should submit to their husbands in everything.

Husbands, love your wives, as Christ loved the church. He gave himself up for her. . . . Husbands should love their wives as they do their own bodies. He who loves his wife loves himself. Observe that no one ever hates his own flesh; no, he nourishes it and takes care of it as Christ cares for the church (Eph. 5:22-29). These words of Saint Paul have been the subject of much controversy down through the centuries and especially in recent years. The reaction of "liberated" people is familiar to all of us. "Wives submit to their husbands! Don't be absurd. That stuff went out with slavery. This is the twentieth century. Why should anyone listen to some male chauvinist who lived at a time when women were treated like dirt?"

Saint Paul needs a good public relations firm, for the implication of his words is not what his modern critics would have you believe. He never said or implied that wives were inferior to their husbands. What he did say was that wives should serve their husbands as the Church serves Christ, and that husbands should love their wives as Christ loved the Church. How did Christ show his love for his Church? He suffered and died for it in the greatest demonstration of love the world has ever known.

The true meaning of Saint Paul's words is that Christian marriage symbolizes the intimate relationship between Christ and the Church, that wives should serve their husbands in the same spirit that the Church serves Christ, and that husbands should care for their wives with the same devotion that our Lord has for his Church. What other analogy could Saint Paul have used that would have conferred higher praise on husbands and wives?

A true wife, then, submits to her husband by her own free decision, not as a result of any demand from him. She trusts her husband completely and is quite happy to follow him. She is an inspiring companion, praising her spouse when he wins a battle, consoling him when he suffers defeat or disappointment, but always encouraging him and demonstrating her faith in him. A good wife is always careful, however, to inspire her husband so that he grows spiritually and emotionally, rather than pushing him only to gain material benefits for them.

The wife's vocation is motherhood. By nature she is ordained for physical and spiritual motherhood. God has entrusted to her the sublime task of bringing children into the world, of fostering the child during its formative years, of guiding it and becoming a loving friend and confidant of her offspring. That is why the Creator gave women such an abundance of tenderness and compassion. A wife is also a manager, a teacher, a nurse, and a creative and versatile playmate for her children. Add to this her role as a gracious and thoughtful helpmate for her husband and you will know why wives are very special people. And husbands are very lucky to have them, as an inspired author of the Old Testament noted centuries ago:

Happy the husband of a good wife, twice-lengthened are his days; a worthy wife brings joy to her husband, peaceful and full is his life. A good wife is a generous gift bestowed upon him who fears the Lord; be he rich or poor, his heart is content, and a smile is ever on his face (Sir. 26:1-4).

The husband's vocation is leadership. Man, in the ordinary providence of God, was meant to be master of the home. A husband, as the leader of his family, must be strong; he must be dominant, but not domineering; he must be a good provider, a teacher to his children, and a source of inspiration to his wife. He must recognize the spiritual and emotional needs of his wife and children and strive always to fulfill these needs. Words of praise and encouragement should never be far from his lips.

God has entrusted to husbands the serious responsibility of caring for and protecting mother and child. They must be able to look to him to solve the problems and overcome the trials in their lives. He will consult with his wife, but he must make the decisions and carry them out. He must be the head of the family in every sense of the word, just as his wife is the heart of the family.

Intellectual processes.   It is important for couples to realize that husbands and wives think in a different way and arrive at conclusions by different thought processes. Men ordinarily follow cold, solid reasoning, somewhat devoid of sentiment, when seeking the solution to a problem. Women usually follow spontaneous, sympathetic intuition. They are more sensitive to another's sentiments and feelings; they are attentive to details.

We do not mean to imply that a woman never reasons logically. Rather we are saying that she reaches conclusions without thinking a matter out systematically. A judgment on her part is mingled with feelings and imagination. But the interesting thing is that she is very often correct in spite of rushing through reasoning to reach conclusions quickly. Those who scoff at a woman's intuition would do well to look at the record and to consider her almost uncanny ability to arrive at the right answer in many situations. When a problem arises, a man will slowly, by logical steps, seek a solution. A woman, on the other hand, will be prompted by her intuition to follow the most advantageous course spontaneously. A man, once having logically reached a solution, is slow to change his mind. A woman is more adaptable.

A man leans toward the abstract in his thinking, a woman towards the concrete. A father is more apt to insist on invariable abstract rules or norms in dealing with his children, while a mother adapts herself according to circumstances. Thus father says that Mary can never go out on a school night; mother realizes that there might be a particular set of circumstances when it will be all right for Mary to go out.

These distinctive intellectual qualities in a husband and wife, strange as it may seem, actually complement each other. If there is mutual understanding of these differences between man and woman, friction will not result and couples will use them in a harmonious way to promote the good of the family.

Emotional natures.   The differences between men and women extend also to their emotions. A woman is blessed with a sensitive nature. She is moved to pleasure, sadness, fear, or anxiety by what, to a husband, are trifles. Ask her to explain her reaction and she cannot. She has a lively imagination, whereas a man leans more towards solid facts, with little reliance on his feelings. A woman will more readily laugh at anything that is amusing and cry at the drop of a handkerchief. A man, by nature, is attracted by this emotional responsiveness; a woman is attracted by the firmness and steadfastness of the man.

In the realm of love and affection, as we noted earlier, a woman seeks to be loved, to have constant affection and attention showered on her. This is especially true when she is pregnant and frequently just after the birth of a child, when many women experience "post-partum blues." At these times, husbands must outdo themselves in tenderness and consideration. Women also desire to give themselves completely in love, in wholehearted sacrifice, in total devotion. A husband's love may be just as deep, but it is less external or expressive. A man seeks someone to love; a woman seeks someone who will love her. To summarize what we have said:

MAN IS CHARACTERIZED

from the physical aspect	by	strength
from the intellectual aspect	by	logic and reason
from the emotional aspect	by	protective love
		stability

WOMAN IS CHARACTERIZED

from the physical aspect	by	gentleness
from the intellectual aspect	by	intuition
from the emotional aspect	by	desire to love
		responsiveness
		sensitivity

FOR BETTER OR FOR WORSE?

The Polish have an old proverb: "Before going to war, pray; before going to sea, pray twice; before getting married, pray three times." This proverb simply recognizes the fact that marriage is one of the most serious steps in one's life and that God must have a part in it from beginning to end. "Unless the Lord build the house," the psalmist said, "they labor in vain who build it" (Ps. 127:1). Young couples about to establish a home and a family must not ignore this sound advice.

When couples approach the altar on their wedding day, they have stars in their eyes. They can see nothing but good times and happy experiences ahead of them. It is doubtful that this rosy outlook ever paled even when the priest instructed newlyweds that the future, "with its hopes and disappointments, its successes and its failures, its pleasures and its pains, its joys and its sorrows, is hidden from your eyes. You know that these elements are mingled in every life, and are to be expected in your own. And so, not knowing what is before you, you take each other for better or for worse, for richer or for poorer, in sickness and in health, until death."

Newlyweds seldom think about problems that might arise in the future. Or if they do think about them, they merely assume that they will be able to cope with such problems when the time comes. And if they try to live up to the Christian ideals of marriage, if God is an important factor in their lives, and if they have tried to develop a deep love for and mutual understanding of each other, there is a good chance that their marriage will turn out for better and not for worse.

But what if in the course of time one party finds himself or herself joined to a partner in marriage for worse instead of for better? Perhaps the husband has become an alcoholic, or is running around with another woman, or is gambling away his week's pay. Or maybe the wife has become a nagging shrew, or has ballooned to an enormous weight, or has decided to "liberate" herself from her domestic responsibilities. What then?

Or suppose one spouse is horribly crippled in an automobile accident, or suffers a severe mental breakdown, or is afflicted with a chronic disease, or they have a badly deformed or retarded child who requires constant care. What happens to that glorious picture of marriage they shared on their wedding day?

The immediate answer of the "media people" is divorce. They say that no person should have to remain in a marriage that has gone sour; that no one should do anything unless he can get something out of it; that

God does not expect any person to live in such an unhappy situation. The "media people" conveniently ignore the words of Christ: "If a man wishes to come after me, he must deny his very self, take up his cross, and begin to follow in my footsteps" (Mt. 16:24). They are so self-centered and selfish that they look with disbelief at those people who, in the words of Saint Francis, do not "so much seek to be consoled as to console; to be understood as to understand; to be loved as to love."

Many a cross in marriage can be borne and survived if deep spiritual and Christian love is present. The cross may be a blessing in disguise. The patient and courageous bearing of that cross may bring a shower of graces on the one willing to bear it, and perhaps even the reform of the other party. There have been many cases of sincere and loving spouses following the advice of Saint Paul: "Help carry one another's burdens; in that way you will fulfill the law of Christ" (Gal. 6:2).

The humble acceptance of crosses, trials, and sufferings can be of tremendous spiritual value, not only in large difficulties but also in the small problems and annoyances of each day. Little by little, husbands and wives can learn to see the hand of God in every part of their lives. A harsh remark, a child's sickness, a spoiled dinner, difficulties at work — all are permitted by God and can be offered up in a spirit of sacrifice and love. Every situation, large or small, can be a means of bringing the family closer to the model of the Holy Family.

If crosses should come in married life, the answer is not to sever the bond, for God has made that permanent. The answer is to unite these crosses with Christ to sanctify yourself, to make you a spiritually better and stronger person, to help your children, to convert and redeem your spouse. Great love can do it as it has done it in the past. "The unbelieving husband is consecrated by his believing wife; the unbelieving wife is consecrated by her believing husband," Saint Paul has said (1 Cor. 7:14).

The Apostle also had good reason for comparing the love of husband and wife to the love of Christ for his Church. Christ delivered himself up, gave himself completely for the Church and for us. So some wives and husbands are asked to make great sacrifices. They cannot make them unless they call on God for help. "Apart from me you can do nothing," our Lord has told us (Jn. 15:5). The answer to great trials or petty difficulties in marriage is not to give up or to become embittered; it is to recognize the faults and failings in each spouse, to make the most of the good things and to accept the bad, and to work and pray for a marital relationship that will provide some true happiness here and eternal happiness hereafter.

One young couple of our acquaintance has a very beautiful custom based on real love and Christ-like understanding. Before each meal, the husband says grace and then kisses his wife. Only after this ritual do they sit down at the table for a meal. This custom is practiced whether there are visitors for dinner or not. No petty difficulty can last for long when such a calling on God and the expressing of mutual love are an intimate part of every day. The same can be said of couples who pray and frequent the sacraments together. The closer a couple is to Christ, the closer they are to a happy and holy marriage.

A ONE HUNDRED PER CENT PROPOSITION

The task of making a success of marriage rests on both husband and wife. It is not a fifty-fifty proposition, as some people contend, but a full-time task that demands one hundred per cent from both spouses. "Success in marriage," says a time-honored proverb, "means not only finding the right mate but also being the right mate." A good test of a marriage is to ask each partner who gives the most to the marriage. If both partners give credit to the other, they have a happy and successful marriage.

A happy marriage does not eliminate all of life's problems, but it can make them more bearable. Certainly a house full of harmony and happiness is smiled upon by God. In the words of the Old Testament: "With three things I am delighted, for they are pleasing to the Lord and to men: Harmony among brethren, friendship among neighbors, and the mutual love of husband and wife" (Sir. 25:1).

CHAPTER 5

Between Parent and Child

> Children are really the supreme gift of marriage and contribute
> very substantially to the welfare of their parents. . . . Parents
> should regard as their proper mission the task of transmitting
> human life and educating those to whom it has been transmitted.
> — Vatican II, *Pastoral Constitution on the Church in the Mod-
> ern World,* No. 50

J. Edgar Hoover, director of the Federal Bureau of Investigation, once said
that the "American home is still the basis of our social order, and the nation will never be any stronger than the home. The one thing that most juvenile criminals have in common is a lack of proper home training. There
is no character building agency to take the place of a good home."

It is indeed true that the family is the basic unit of society, and its influence on the well-being of the individual, the Church, and the nation is
widely recognized. The importance of the family extends into many fields,
but when we look at the proper mission of the family as established by
God, namely, the procreation and training of children, then we must acknowledge that the relation of the family to youth is of the highest importance. The training and attitudes which are conveyed to young people
within the family circle will affect significantly the future of our Church
and our country.

Unfortunately, we must concede at the outset that everything is not as
it should be with the family today. There are serious problems to face and
Christian parents and children should take the lead in facing and solving
them. Alcoholism, crime, drugs, juvenile criminality, mental illness, suicide, lack of respect for authority, and the weakened influence of religion
are troubles only too familiar to the present generation of children and
adults. These problems have always existed, of course, but never have they

At the father's death,
he will seem not dead, since
he leaves after him one
like himself.
— (Sir. 30:4).

photo by Paul J. Hayes

been so widespread, never have they seemed so overwhelming, never has the response to them seemed so timid and uncertain.

Even good parents do not seem anxious to make the necessary effort to protect their children from these problems or to bring the level of family life up to the Christian ideal. Instead, some parents, perhaps without even realizing it, seem resigned to lowering the level of family life to pagan depths. They have lost their will to fight. They are like the man walking along the street who saw a drunkard lying in the gutter. The man looked at the drunkard for a minute and then said: "I can't lift you up, but I tell you what I'll do. I'll lie down beside you!"

So often, sincere parents look over the present situation among youth — their attendance at degrading and dirty movies, their use of foul language, their reading of immoral books and magazines, their attachment to alcohol and drugs, their involvement in early and prolonged sexual experiences, their contempt for the property and possessions of others — and then, with a shrug of the shoulders, say, "Oh, well, young people are different these days. I guess I can't be too strict with my children."

We are not implying that all young people fall into these categories. There are many boys and girls who are a credit to their families, their Church, and their God. But even these children find it increasingly more difficult to buck the tide of immorality and licentiousness. They are often subjected to ridicule and scorn and even physical abuse for not doing what "everybody else" is doing. These children need the support and encouragement and example of a true Christian family to do the right thing in a society that is intent on doing the wrong thing. With the proper education and training at home, Catholic boys and girls can become witnesses to Christ in the world. They can let the light of his teachings shine before their friends and acquaintances in a pagan society. This is their mission and the mission of every follower of Christ.

In order to deal with the problems confronted by parents and children, it is necessary to discuss the purpose of the family and the roles and duties entrusted to mothers, fathers, and children by God himself. Only by starting from the foundations and working up can we draw a blueprint for the ideal Christian family.

THE PURPOSE OF THE FAMILY

It is and always has been the teaching of the Catholic Church that a prime purpose of the institution of marriage is the begetting and upbringing of children. In the words of Vatican II: "The true practice of conjugal love, and the whole meaning of the family life which results from it, have this aim: that the couple be ready with stout hearts to cooperate with the love of the Creator and the Savior, who through them will enlarge and enrich his own family day by day" (*Pastoral Constitution on the Church in the Modern World,* No. 50).

What an exalted vocation marriage and family life is! God could have decided to bring new lives into the world by direct creation as he did with Adam and Eve. But instead, he chose to have human beings work in partnership with him. A man and wife have a unique position in God's scheme of things. They cooperate with God in creation. The parents work with God in producing the body; he produces the soul. Marriage cannot accomplish this fundamental purpose without the contribution of Almighty God.

Cardinal Richard J. Cushing, Archbishop of Boston, once observed that "our young people are the most important people in the world." This very simple but significant statement points up another purpose of the family: the upbringing and training of children. Husbands and wives not only share in the creation of children with God, but they must then work with God to educate and prepare their children for their proper role in life.

People make headlines today if they discover a new medicine to cure a deadly disease, if they write a best-selling book, if they pitch a no-hitter in the World Series, or if they win a tennis championship. Prominent people from all walks of life are held in esteem. But their accomplishments pale into insignificance when compared with the task of training a soul for God, of joining with God in bringing new souls into the world and molding them according to the plan of God for their eventual return to him. Children are the truly important people of our day and our hope for the future.

The Christian family should be a team, with each member having certain responsibilities to fulfill. When one or more members of a baseball team neglect their duties and fail to execute their proper role, the team runs into trouble. The same is true of the family. In the game of life, however, the consequences of poor teamwork are far more devastating than those experienced in an athletic event. Hence the need for spelling out the duties and responsibilities of each member of the family. Only when these roles are fully understood and faithfully lived will the family be strong enough to bring about the Christianization of our society.

THE ROLE OF PARENTS

The goal of Christian parents must be to help their children to become

Christian men and women in the fullest sense. To have any hope of accomplishing this goal, parents must first of all be completely Christian themselves. They must be models worthy of imitation by their children. The importance of good example, of practicing what you preach, can never be overemphasized. It is not enough for parents to point out the way to their children; they must lead the way. If they want their children to pray, they must pray; if they want their children to go to church, they must go to church; if they want their boys and girls to be truthful and honest, parents must be truthful and honest; if they want them to respect the name of God and refrain from cursing, they must do likewise; if they want their children to read decent literature and watch wholesome movies and television programs, parents must not violate these conditions themselves.

The most obvious role of parents is that of providing children with the necessities of life — food, shelter, clothing, medical care, education, and so forth. All of these things are important in giving a child a sense of security and well-being. Children must be taught, however, the value and proper use of the material goods of this world. They must never get the idea that life is just one long pursuit of material wealth. They must be encouraged early and often to thank God for the material blessings that have come their way. They must be told of their obligation as followers of Christ to share their earthly goods with those who are less fortunate. "I assure you," our Lord said, "as often as you did it for one of my least brothers, you did it for me" (Mt. 25:40).

Parents must give their children love and affection. There is a story of a little girl named Laura who lived in an orphanage. Her playmates often made fun of her because of an unsightly birthmark on her face, and so Laura preferred to play by herself. One day, one of the teachers at the orphanage saw the little girl climb the fence that enclosed the property, reach over the top, and place an envelope on the branch of a tree just beyond the fence. After Laura had returned to the building where she lived, the teacher retrieved the envelope. In it was a note with these words: "To anybody who reads this, I love you! Laura."

Children crave love and affection. If they do not find these feelings at home, they will seek them outside the home. The mutual love of parents for their offspring can have a great influence on children. This love and affection can be shown in many ways. It may consist of understanding and support for children; it may involve giving them a sense of worth and self-esteem; it may mean openness and sympathy, advice and direction, encouragement in their school work or in their hobbies, and respect for their privacy, their good reputation, their personal religious life, and their choice of vocation.

Whether by word or deed, parents must communicate their love to their children. They must, in fact, just plain communicate. They must be approachable, they must show an interest in what their children are saying, they must answer their questions honestly and fully, they must listen, listen, listen. There should be family conversation times, as well as opportunities for private talks. Parents should never refuse a child's request for a private conversation. It is through open and honest dialogue that children will gain confidence in their parents, and parents will gain confidence in their children.

Not every conversation between parents and children will result in complete agreement on both sides. All opinions should be voiced in a spirit of charity, and once a decision is reached, the discussion should be terminated. Children will find some decisions hard to accept, but if they feel that their parents have been open and fair and attentive to their views, they will usually abide by whatever decisions are reached. It is when parents refuse even to discuss a matter in a candid and reasonable way that unhealthy conflicts arise in the family and children feel less and less inclined to seek parental advice about some problem or situation that has arisen.

THE ROLE OF CHILDREN

Just as parents have certain duties and responsibilities to their children, so children have duties and responsibilities to their parents. There is no one, with the exception of God, to whom children owe more loyalty and devotion than their parents. The parents who, from the day they were born, have fed, clothed, sheltered, and educated them, have taken care of them when they were sick, and have given them just about everything they could ever reasonably want or need. It is doubtful that most children could ever do as much for their parents as has been done for them.

The best way that children can repay their parents is by always showing them love, respect, and obedience, especially when they disagree on something, and by taking time now and then to say thank you. They can repay their parents by discussing things with them, asking their advice, keeping them informed of their activities, and generally being open and honest with them. Genuine communication is a two-way street. Children who expect their parents to listen to them must listen to their parents. They must be polite and courteous, understanding and patient. When discussion has ended and a decision has been made, children must accede to their parents' wishes, because parents stand in the place of God. In the words of Saint Paul: "Children, obey your parents in the Lord, for that is what is expected of you. 'Honor your father and mother' is the first commandment to carry a promise with it — 'that it may go well with you, and that you may have long life on the earth' " (Eph. 6:1-3).

Children who keep open the lines of communication with their parents and with their brothers and sisters will avoid many of the problems and heartaches which plague so many young people today.

Children also should help mom and dad with the household chores — making the beds, cleaning the house, doing the dishes, preparing the meals, mowing the lawn, running errands, taking care of the younger children, and so forth. These chores should be done automatically and voluntarily and not only after mom or dad has to yell or threaten to take away some privilege. These tasks are not always pleasant, but neither is getting up for work every morning or washing clothes or putting three meals on the table. Doing chores willingly and with a smile might not make them any more pleasant, but it will go a long way toward making your house a happy home.

To sum up the roles of the members of a family, we can turn to the warm and kindly Pope John XXIII:

Let the father of the family take the place of God among his children, and not only by his authority but by the upright example of his life also stand clearly in the first place.

Let the mother, however, rule firmly and agreeably over her offspring by gentleness and virtue in the domestic setting. Let her behave with indulgence and love towards her husband, and along with him, let her carefully instruct and train her family, the most precious gift given by God.

The children are always to obey the parents who bore them, as is fitting, and love them, and be to them not only a comfort, but, in time of need, a real support.

Within the walls of the home let there be that warmth of love which existed in the family at Nazareth (*Ad Petri Cathedram*, June 29, 1959).

THE EDUCATION AND TRAINING OF CHILDREN

There is no educational institution more important for a child than the family. No school can compensate for what is lacking there. The home is the natural education element and the parent is the teacher appointed by God. In the words of Vatican II: "Parents must be acknowledged as the first and foremost educators of their children. Their role as educators is so decisive that scarcely anything can compensate for their failure in it" (*Declaration on Christian Education*, No. 3).

The task of training children and transmitting values to them in today's society is an awesome one. It begins at birth and continues until children become of age or make a home for themselves. The task belongs to both parents and is one more reason against divorce. The upbringing of children cannot be safeguarded except through a stable marriage bond.

We do not exaggerate when we say that a child's training must begin at birth. A famous prison warden once observed that "it is in the high chair not the electric chair that crime must be fought." And psychologists assure us that a child is pretty well formed by the age of six. These pre-school years are vitally important and should be a matter of serious thought and concern for parents.

The family is the first and best school of faith and morals because it is there that children first learn of God, learn to love him and pray to him, learn of the Church, learn the wholesomeness of human companionship, and learn to love their neighbor. Or at least children will learn these things if their parents are oriented toward God in their daily lives. In a truly Catholic family, the word "God" should be as familiar to children as "mom" and "dad."

As soon as children begin to understand, prayers should be taught and stories told of God and Jesus, Mary and the saints. Small children find Bible stories fascinating and religious and moral principles can be taught by reading to them of God the Creator, Adam and Eve, Moses, Daniel, and, of course, the events in the life of Jesus. Children will have many questions about these stories and about God. Parents can use these opportunities to impart a world of valuable knowledge about God and our relationship with him to their youngsters at a time when their minds are like sponges, just waiting to soak up information. Parents who neglect these important years may regret it later when they are confronted by teenagers who have little or no interest in God or his Church.

When the time comes for children to enter school, Catholic parents have the duty "to entrust their children to Catholic schools, when and where this is possible, to support such schools to the extent of their ability, and to work along with them for the welfare of their children" (*Declaration on Christian Education*, No. 8). Where Catholic schools are not available, parents should enroll their children in parish programs of religious education, and should become involved in these programs themselves.

Parents cannot completely delegate the religious education of their children to any school or program whatsoever. The role of the parent as a religious educator does not cease when a child enters school. The parent must continue the training and moral formation of the child at home and make sure that the child's classroom instruction does not contradict or undermine correct doctrine or sound morality. Parents should also take advantage of good Catholic literature and adult education courses to keep themselves informed and prepared to teach their children.

Among the spiritual duties of parents is the obligation to pray for and with their children. The power of prayer can be astounding. Many problems could be solved if some of the time spent in undue concern and anger was devoted to prayer. Saint Monica had a problem child, the future Saint Augustine. She prayed for him for many long years and through those prayers saw him return to God from whom he had drifted far.

Family life should be one constant prayer, from the Morning Offering, to grace before and after meals, to the family rosary, to evening prayers and spiritual readings. The family that prays together stays together. Important, too, is frequent recourse to the sacraments — Mass and Communion regularly, Confession frequently. This daily striving for holiness cannot help but make the duties and responsibilities of family life easier to shoulder.

Since we have mentioned the sacraments, parents should be reminded of their important spiritual duty of having a child baptized promptly. Following upon this is the obligation to arrange for a child's First Penance, First Communion, and Confirmation, and to take an active part in the child's preparation for these sacraments. With proper instruction and encouragement from parents, these sacramental encounters with Christ can be joyous and fruitful occasions for children that will stay with them for the rest of their lives.

Finally, parents and guardians are bound to observe and correct youths entrusted to their care. To put this in a practical light, it means, for instance, to supervise the children's homework and school work, to know who their friends are, to find out where they are going when they leave the house. Any mother or father who takes the attitude that as long as there is peace and quiet in the house, little effort need be made to find out where their boys or girls are, or with whom they are spending their time, or what they are doing, will be answerable to God for neglecting important parental responsibilities.

Parents must check what their children are reading, what television shows they are watching, what movies they are attending. Parents who are indifferent to having their children read morally objectionable books and magazines, or view filthy and degrading programs and films, share in the guilt. Massive quantities of morally objectionable materials pour out in a polluted stream each year. Adults are bound before God not only to avoid such materials themselves but to steer their children away from them, too.

This obligation of correction and training is by no means easy, and that is all the more reason why parents should rely on prayer and the sacraments to seek God's special help in this all-important job. With God's help parents can be just, merciful, patient, and considerate in dealing with their children.

DISCIPLINE

Failure to discipline a child and to show him that he cannot always have his own way is no favor to the child. When an undisciplined child runs into serious difficulties, and finds that these difficulties cannot be resolved immediately, he often becomes angry and even violent. He is so used to having his own way that he cannot tolerate resistance to his demands.

Children need and want limits. It is vital for their security and well-being that they know what is expected of them, what the boundaries are which govern their activities. Limits, boundaries, and expectations must be pointed out very early in a child's life and then the reins can be loosened as the child grows older and more mature.

Discipline to be effective must be fair, firm, consistent, and constructive. *Fair* means that the punishment should fit the crime. *Firm* means that the punishment should be decisively and promptly administered. *Consistent* means that the same infraction should always be treated in the same way, not punished one time and overlooked another; not resulting in an easy punishment for one child and a harsh sentence for another. It also means that both parents agree on the disciplinary system, and support each other in its enforcement. *Constructive* means that discipline should not be strictly negative. An explanation of the bad conduct should accompany the punishment so that the child can learn from the experience.

Finally, discipline must be balanced with love. Just as a husband and wife should not let disagreements and conflicts carry over until the next day, so parents should not allow children to go to sleep at night without discussing the incident or without expressing their continued love and affection for the offender. Parental firmness does no psychological harm to children. On the contrary, it shows youngsters that parents really care about them.

A word of advice to parents and future parents: Children respond to praise much quicker than they do to criticism. Establish a system of rules and responsibilities for the family, and enforce it. But do not constantly nag the children about little things. And when they are good, reward them with praise, affection, treats, and extra privileges. Children generally aim to please their parents and win their approval, so frequent expressions of that approval will accomplish more than constant criticism and ridicule. Firm leadership coupled with love, understanding, and patience will result in happier and well-behaved offspring and a peaceful family.

SEX EDUCATION — WHEN, WHAT, AND HOW MUCH?

There are few matters more controversial today than education in human sexuality. People are generally agreed on the need for sex education for children, but they are far apart when it comes to the best way of meeting this very important need. Some feel that it should be the exclusive prerogative of parents; others that the schools ought to help out. Some feel that the moral dimensions of sexuality must be included; others say that morality should have little or nothing to do with it, that only clinical details and contraceptive techniques should be presented.

What does the Church expect of Catholic parents in this sensitive area? It expects, in the words of Vatican II, that as children advance in years, they will be given "positive and prudent sexual education" (*Declaration on Christian Education*, No. 1). The Catholic Bishops of the United States expanded on this instruction in 1972, declaring that parents are "primarily responsible for imparting to their children an awareness of the sacredness of sexuality" (*To Teach as Jesus Did*, No. 56).

The bishops went on to say that "the child's need for and right to adequate knowledge and guidance, adapted to his age and individual maturity, are the paramount considerations. In all programs proper emphasis must be given to the spiritual and moral dimensions of sexuality. The child's reverence for the God-given dignity and beauty of sex is an effective safeguard of purity; it should be cultivated from the earliest years" (*To Teach as Jesus Did*, No. 58).

It is not within the scope of this book to offer detailed instructions on how to educate children in human sexuality; sound literature along these lines is readily available.* However, we would like to offer a few basic thoughts and suggestions.

1.   Normally, the best sex educators of children are their parents. Parents are more readily available to their children when they have questions; they know better than anyone else when children are in need of instruction; they can deal with each child on an informal and individual basis; they can, through their own healthy attitudes toward sex, give their children a healthy attitude.

2.   Sex education is a long-term and continuing process.

3.   Keep the instruction simple and truthful. The instruction does not have to be perfect.

4.   Mere physical facts are not enough. Moral formation of children is more important than just giving them information. Providing children with explicit factual information about sex, while ignoring the moral and spiritual aspects, can only lead to trouble.

5.   Encourage modesty in dress and respect and reverence for the body. This is probably the most important thing that parents can do to give their children a Christian outlook on sex, and it will also be the most difficult. In a society in which the undraped, or partially draped human body is used to sell everything from apples to zucchini, it is not easy to teach children that their bodies are special and that modesty is a virtue to be greatly desired and constantly practiced. But conscientious Catholic parents, recognizing that the follower of Christ must be different, will, by word and example, hold the Christian ideal of sexuality ever before their offspring. Having vaccinated their children against disease, they will also vaccinate them against a sick philosophy of sex.

PARENTHOOD MEANS SACRIFICE

There was a story in the newspapers not long ago of an eight-year-old boy who fought his way three miles through deep snow to a neighbor's house to seek help for his·mother, who lay dying at home. Help was obtained, the mother was rushed to a hospital, and her life was saved. "It was one of the most remarkable things I've ever seen a boy do," the neighbor said.

The point of the story is that parents never know how their children

*For example: *Your Child and Sex* by Msgr. George A. Kelly; *How to Teach Children the Wonder of Sex* by Dr. and Mrs. J. C. Willke, and *In the Image of God* by Sean O'Reilly, M.D.

will react in certain situations. Mothers and fathers can only give their offspring good example and good training, teach them to love God and their neighbor, to treat others as they would like to be treated — and pray. Having done all of these things, parents can then stand before God and say that they did all they could to return to God this soul entrusted to their care.

The task of parenthood requires all-out service and sacrifice. In a world where men and women are brought up surrounded by an attitude of selfishness and individualism, parents need gallant hearts that dare to be different. But any goal worth obtaining means sacrifice and daring to do what is right instead of what everyone else is doing. And the goal of a successful family life surpasses the earthly success of any other human endeavor. A good home, where rights and duties of both parents and children are honored, comes as close to earthly paradise as anything we might hope for in this life.

A false picture, a caricature, of marriage and the family is being presented to us today by the pleasure-seekers in our society. We must be on guard not to be influenced by this phony portrait. The sooner the world gets back to the true Christian ideals of marriage and the family, to the recognition and realization of the primary purpose of the family — the cooperation with God in the procreation and education of youth — the better it will be for the world.

Saint Francis de Sales gives this important bit of advice: "Parents ought often to speak of God to their children, but yet more often to speak to God of their children."

Family life is important. Christ himself spent thirty out of his thirty-three years on earth in the midst of a family. The ideal of Christian family life was set by Jesus, Mary, and Joseph in Nazareth.

But Nazareth is on a hill, and you have to climb to get there.

191. Which are the chief com...
The chief comm...
1. To h...
2. ...

...nich are the commandments of God?

The commandments of God are these ten:

1. I am the Lord thy God; thou shalt not have strange gods before Me.
2. Thou shalt not take the name of the Lord thy God in vain.
3. Remember thou keep holy the Lord's day.
4. Honor thy father and thy mother.
5. Thou shalt not kill.
6. Thou shalt not commit adultery.
7. Thou shalt not steal.
8. Thou shalt not bear false witness against thy neighbor.
9. Thou shalt not covet thy neighbor's wife.
10. Thou shalt not covet thy neighbor's goods.

...we be satisfied merely to keep the command-
...f God?

...uld not be satisfied merely to keep the ...ments of God, but should always be ...ds, even when they are

...Our Saviour especially recommend that is ...commanded by the law of God?

...ur especially recommends the ob-...ce of the Evangelical Counsels — vol-...tary poverty, perpetual chastity, and per-fect obedience.

HOLY BIBLE

CHAPTER 6

Authority and Love

Young persons exert very substantial influence on modern society. . . . They themselves ought to become the prime and direct apostles of youth, exercising the apostolate among themselves and through themselves and reckoning with the social environment in which they live. — Vatican II, *Decree on the Apostolate of the Laity,* No. 12

From the time of Adam the raising of children has been a difficult task, particularly during the teenage years. The reason for this is simple: parents and children come from different generations and tend to view their situations from different perspectives. This so-called "gap" will cause no more than the usual disagreements and annoyances if parents and children maintain a mutual respect, understanding, consideration, and love for each other.

The rearing of teenagers is more complicated for parents today, however, because of increasing pressures and influences from outside the family. These may come from teachers, from the children's peers, or from the mass media, especially from television, which some observers have termed "the third parent" in the average family. It is a fact that by the time a child reaches the age of 16, he or she will have spent about 15,000 to 20,000 hours in front of the television set. Imagine if the Church could have this much influence over the development of a child!

When you consider, too, the kinds of information and propaganda that are conveyed to the child by television, is it any wonder that parents find it hard to develop Christian attitudes in their offspring?

Parents who are sincere about educating and training their children must realize that outside influences, not all of them good, have a terrific impact on the development of their teenagers. Parents must do all they can, therefore, to screen out the bad influences as much as possible and increase their own good influence, and that of the Church, on their sons and daughters. This is one of their first and foremost duties. Taking such steps will frequently pit responsible Catholic parents against friends, neighbors, and society, but parents must have confidence in their own judgment and the courage of their convictions. For only they, not friends, neighbors, or society, will have to answer to God for the way in which their children were brought up.

THE CRISIS OF AUTHORITY

The revolt against authority has reached frightening levels today. Christians have to be concerned at the widespread contempt for authority, a contempt that has infected many teenagers and even children in their preteen years. The situation that exists in many of our schools today, where the ABC's have come to mean assaults, burglaries, and crimes, is just one illustration of the problem that exists. Nor has the Christian family been immune from this disease, and it is in the family that the revolt must be stopped first if we hope to correct the situation in society at large.

What do we mean by authority? *Authority is the right to command and enforce obedience.* In the family, authority is the foundation of discipline. Without it, family life would be chaotic. It is vitally important, however, that we not neglect to mention the place of love in this picture. Authority with love is a firm but gentle molding of a child's character after the pattern of Jesus Christ.

Parents, by training and experience, know more than their children and are their offspring's most important advisors. What a tragedy it is when there is little or no communication between parents and children, and the opportunity is lost for mutual understanding and sharing of each other's burdens. Those who have survived the trials of adolescence should sympathize with the new generation of teenagers and do all they can to help their sons and daughters to come through this unique experience as painlessly as possible.

Another point worthy of note is that most teenagers like their parents even though they would have trouble telling them so. Teenagers should show their love for their parents. Why hide it? Just as the love of a husband and wife can wither if it is not expressed, so too with the love between parents and children. And express your love now; do not procrastinate until you find yourself at the funeral of your mother or father, wishing that you had another chance to tell them how much they meant to you.

Authority does not have to be the bugaboo that many people make it out to be. Teenagers want parental supervision. They need limits and boundaries. They can handle only so much freedom and they crave the security of knowing what is expected of them. They will rebel at times, and concerned and loving parents, exercising the authority given to them by God, will stand firm, while at the same time trying to see and understand the teenager's point of view. Teenagers will then respect and obey and love their parents for being firm but fair in enforcing discipline.

The general guideline in these situations is that parents should be strict enough to keep children in line, and lenient enough to allow them to make some decisions for themselves — and to allow them to take the consequences when their decisions do not turn out as expected. Parents make a mistake when they try to remove or cushion all the bumps on the road of their teenager's life, for they give their child a false picture of life and ill prepare him for adulthood. We all learn from the rough spots on the road of life, and no child should be raised with the idea that life is just one long, wide, and smooth superhighway. Parents must be honest and truthful with their children if they expect to gain their trust and confidence.

There is a story about a 20-year-old man who was discussing his parents with a friend. "You know," he said, "when I was 16, my father didn't know anything. And today he knows quite a bit. It's amazing how much he learned in just four years." After the son had made a few mistakes of his own, he began to realize that none of us is perfect and that perhaps his father was a pretty smart individual after all.

It is too bad that so many parents and children have to go through these difficult stages before they come to appreciate and understand each other. Let us turn to four problem areas in the life of teenagers and offer some guidelines to parents and adolescents that might be helpful in facing and solving these problems in a Christian manner. The troublesome areas might be classified as the "Four D's" — Dating, Drinking, Drugs, and Driving.

THE TEENAGER AND DATING

We know very little about the life of Saint Valentine, except that he was martyred for his faith in the third century. How he became the patron saint of lovers, why we exchange tender notes on the fourteenth of February every year, are questions whose answers have been lost in the misty corridors of time. What we do know, however, is that young people will be attracted to each other, will exchange love notes, and will be a delight to see when they are together. It was so in the days of Saint Valentine, it is so today, and it will be so until the end of the world.

The romantic attraction between young people of the opposite sex is perfectly natural and good because it is part of the Creator's divine plan. It is only the abuse of the divine plan that should be feared. Parents and teenagers should not be afraid of youthful relationships with the opposite sex. There are many pitfalls to be avoided, to be sure, but on the other hand, wholesome companionship between boys and girls is the beginning of good marriages. To insure such wholesome companionship during the adolescent years, there are some practical norms or words of advice that might be helpful to parents, guardians, and teenagers during these years.

1. *Parents should start with the presumption that their children are morally good and then provide them with all the information they need in the matter of sexuality.* To set a child adrift in the sex-saturated modern world without any moral guidance from the home is an outrage. Positive and prudent sex education should begin in the home, by word and example, long before a child enters school. It should be expanded and adapted to the child's age and maturity.

2. *The youth of today are as confused and unsure of their sexuality as their counterparts of generations gone by.* They have been exposed to a lot more of the facts and terminology and techniques than their predecessors, but few understand and appreciate the place of sex in the divine plan of God. They have been inundated with the physical side of sex but hardly touched at all by the spiritual dimensions. They are easy prey for the purveyors of pornography, permissiveness, promiscuity, perversion, and planned parenthood.

3. *Parents have an obligation to help their teenagers to form their consciences.* This can be done by discussion of moral problems from a common-sense and logical point of view, and through discussion of morality as revealed in the Scriptures and in the teaching of the Catholic Church. It is not enough merely to impart information on sex to young people. The goal should always be *formation* — the cultivation of respect and reverence for the sexual powers given to us by God, and for our bodies as temples of the Holy Spirit. Instead of providing their children with the latest contraceptive drugs or devices, parents should encourage chastity and self-control. The world says that the sexual appetite cannot be controlled; Christianity says that it can, and offers the shining example of millions of its adherents over the centuries as clear evidence of this fact. Young people are very idealistic today and they ought to be given some Christian ideals, instead of

being dragged down to the lowest moral and social common denominator.

4. *Young people need to know that there are objective standards of morality, that the rightness or wrongness of an act does not depend solely on the situation.* The specifics of Christian morality can be found within the overall framework of the Ten Commandments of God and the Sermon on the Mount, especially the Beatitudes. "In the area of sexuality," the Catholic Bishops of the United States have told us, "the Christian is to be modest in behavior and dress. In a sex-saturated society, the follower of Christ must be different. For the Christian there can be no premarital sex, fornication, adultery, or other acts of impurity or scandal to others. He must remain chaste, repelling lustful desires and temptations, self-abuse, pornography, and indecent entertainment of every description" (*Basic Teachings for Catholic Religious Education,* No. 19).

5. *The ground rules for dating ought to be thoroughly discussed and carefully worked out by parents and their teenagers.* Parents ought to know *who* their children are going out with, *what* they intend to do on the date, *when* they will be home, and *where* they are going. Parents seek this information not to pry or snoop but because they love their children and accept the responsibility of watching out for their spiritual and moral well-being. Parents, who were once teenagers themselves, know that there are certain persons (boys and girls of loose morals) and places (drive-in theaters, parked cars, beaches, homes where the parents are out for the evening) that can be occasions of sin for their offspring. They know that sex is a powerful urge, not unlike a runaway locomotive, and that even the strongest-willed teenager will not always be able to resist opportunities and temptations if he or she is confronted with them often enough. Parental supervision means keeping children out of situations where adult decisions will have to be made.

6. *Young people who begin dating in the seventh or eighth or ninth grades are on the road to serious moral trouble.* This would be true even if teenagers today were not exposed to such massive propaganda about the joys and pleasures of sex. The basic reason is too early exposure, on a one-to-one basis, to members of the opposite sex. Individual dating should not begin until at least the junior and senior year of high school, and even then double dating is to be preferred. Prior to that time, boys and girls should involve themselves in group activities — parties, dances, athletic events — all properly chaperoned, of course. This may sound old-fashioned and out of tune with the times, but sensible and honest teenagers will recognize the wisdom of the advice.

7. *"Going steady" is dangerous to the moral, emotional, and intellectual health of teenagers.* By going steady, we mean keeping company exclusively with one person. It is actually the same as the courtship or engagement period in which a man and woman evaluate each other as potential marriage partners for life. So unless a couple is contemplating marriage in the reasonably near future, going steady should be forbidden. There are advantages to going steady, such as never having to worry about getting a date or being lucky enough to have a "steady" who is kind and attentive and fun to be with. But these are outweighed by the disadvantages, including the normal impossibility of avoiding sexual intimacy. The frequent contact cannot help but lead to increased sexual excitement and sexual experimentation. Parents who encourage this kind of exclusive arrangement share responsibility for the sins committed.

Other disadvantages of going steady include the risk of complete dependence on one another, the failure to make new friends, the lack of participation in exciting interests and hobbies because they do not appeal to the other person, the retardation of mental and emotional growth, and the devastated feeling when the relationship that was going to last forever breaks up, as most of them do. Who needs that kind of traumatic experience at the age of 16 or 17? Those who mix with a number of people of both sexes undergo a much more normal development and are much happier.

8. *Premarital sex is not the fulfilling experience that the promoters of promiscuity would have you believe.* The advocates of early and frequent sex never mention the practical problems that have wreaked havoc in the lives of so many young people — the unwanted pregnancies, the staggering number of abortions, the emotional harm, the alarming incidence of venereal disease, the heavy burden of a guilty conscience, the harm to a future marriage. How many boys and girls, urged into premarital sex by the lie that "everybody is doing it," have come away from the experience bitterly disappointed and wishing that they had waited? How many young people have fallen for the oldest line of all — the one that says that sexual intercourse is required to prove the depth of their love? What kind of "love" is it that asks a girl, for example, to give up cheaply the precious gift of her virtue, that exposes her to a possible illegitimate pregnancy, that causes her to abandon her moral convictions, that asks her to jeopardize her eternal salvation? It is not love, of course, it is lust, and the lustful one, having succeeded in his conquest, usually moves on to try the same line on another unsuspecting girl.

9. *Purity is security.* The struggle to attain purity has never been an easy one to win. It is doubly difficult for the youth of today because they see impurity praised and glorified everywhere. We are living in an age where, as someone has said, they stone the virgins instead of the harlots. To resist the pressures of their peers and of the sex pushers in the media, teenagers must build up their moral strength. They must work just as hard to keep their immortal souls in shape as they do to keep their mortal bodies in trim. They can do this, first, by finding out exactly how and when God expects them to use the sexual powers he gave them; second, by forming a right conscience to guide them through the situations they will encounter; third, by giving good example to others and never, by word, action, or provocative dress, leading another person into sin; fourth, by avoiding persons, places, and things that could be occasions of sin; fifth, by concentrating on the development of their personalities, talents, brains, and holiness, rather than their physical and sexual attributes; and sixth, by constantly seeking God's help both to restrain their own passions and to act as his apostles in the modern world.

This divine assistance, without which we can do nothing, can be obtained in many ways: through the Mass, the sacraments of Penance and the Holy Eucharist, prayer, good works, and spiritual reading, especially the Bible. How ironic that so many teenagers neglect these vital sources of help at a time when they need such help the most. With God's grace, purity is within the grasp of young people. And purity is security insofar as it guarantees what sin can never guarantee — true happiness in this life and in the next life.

THE TEENAGER AND DRINKING

If you were to ask a number of people to name the most dangerous drug they know of, you might get such answers as LSD, heroin, cocaine, and so forth. And these certainly are dangerous drugs, but speaking broadly the most dangerous drug of all today is alcohol, because it is socially and legally acceptable even though it is potentially habit-forming and deadly. Alcohol is dangerous because it is involved in 50 per cent of all the crimes committed in the United States, in 50 per cent of all the highway accidents and highway deaths, and in 50 per cent of all the accidents in the home.

There are more than ten million known alcoholics in this country who have brought untold heartache and disaster to themselves, their friends, and society. Furthermore, the problem is not getting better; it is getting worse, especially as heavy drinking moves down the age ladder even into the pre-teen years. It is estimated that at least half a million teenagers are problem drinkers.

Some parents can be heard expressing a sigh of relief at reports that many teenagers are switching from drugs to alcohol. That is like taking consolation from the fact that the person about to mug you is carrying a knife instead of a gun. And how many parents know that some adolescents are mixing alcohol with barbiturates, thus becoming addicted to both drugs?

The teenage alcohol scene is bleak, but it is not hopeless by any means. Conscientious, informed, and prayerful parents and their children can handle the problems of alcohol by facing the facts, discussing the situation calmly and intelligently with each other, and giving good example. Parents and teenagers might consider the following points:

1. *Parents should tell children the truth about alcohol.* Like so many other things, it is not the use of alcohol that is bad, but rather the abuse of it. If the use of alcohol is evil and sinful, would Jesus have changed water into wine at the wedding feast at Cana? Parents who drink should do so moderately. They should indicate to their children that alcohol is one of life's pleasures, not a crutch or the central point of life. Creating the proper attitude at home is very important.

2. *Parents should impress upon their children that teenage drinking is inadvisable and dangerous and should be avoided until the children are of legal age.* In addition to the hazards of alcohol already related, parents ought to stress that alcohol can be a moral danger in that it breaks down religious convictions, dulls the conscience, and often leads to serious sin. Drinking should be taboo for high school students, whatever their age.

3. *The reasons for teenage drinking should be clearly understood and acted upon if necessary.* The most common reasons why young people drink include: a desire for acceptance among their peers; to show how grown up and sophisticated they are; to overcome a feeling of failure or to ease the pain of growing up, and to get high. The first two reasons are neither new nor very profound. They can usually be handled by deglamourizing drinking and the alleged maturity and sophistication it supposedly brings, and by pointing out that peer acceptance is not worth endangering one's physical, emotional, and spiritual health. Unfortunately, these lessons are usually learned the hard way. The third and fourth reasons suggest problems much deeper than the drinking itself and ought to be treated immediately and, if necessary, with professional help.

4. *Teenagers must dare to be different.* They must resist the pres-

sure to drink. They should stay away from those who drink or who have access to alcohol. Those who are of drinking age should never make alcohol available to younger persons, thereby creating problems for other children and their families. People who truly love their neighbor would never do anything to corrupt or destroy another person's life. Teenagers who find themselves with a drinking problem of their own, or in their family, should seek advice and assistance from their priest or reliable relatives, friends, or organizations which specialize in helping those afflicted with alcoholism. Help is always available, of course, from Almighty God if we but ask him.

THE TEENAGER AND DRUGS

In recent years, many parents have been horrified to find that their children, from college age down to the elementary grades, have become confirmed users of drugs. And even though the dangers of hard drugs have been broadcast far and wide, still the number of young people surrendering their bodies and souls to drugs continues to increase.

The teenage drug scene, like the youthful alcohol scene, is frightening, but it can be substantially improved through the mutual efforts of parents and teenagers. Some suggestions:

1. *Parents should be knowledgeable about drugs and drug abuse.* They should communicate this knowledge to their children in an honest and forthright manner, should not abuse alcohol or pills themselves, should confront their children if they recognize signs of drug usage (loss of weight, aches and pains, runny nose, vomiting, unnatural amount of sleep, lack of interest in the things that ordinarily interest boys and girls, and long and deep periods of depression, followed by short periods of elation), and should seek professional help in treating the problem. Parents should also try to find out where the drugs were obtained and inform the local police so that steps may be taken to apprehend the criminals who are selling the narcotics to teenagers.

2. *The reasons for teenage drug usage should be determined and acted upon accordingly.* The reasons for using drugs are basically the same as for drinking: a desire for acceptance; to escape from the problems and failures and disappointments of real life, and to get high. Again, the last two reasons conceal much deeper motivations and demand immediate analysis and treatment. But whatever the reason for drug usage, immediate action is imperative, first, because drugs can enslave and destroy a person much faster than alcohol, and second, because feeding a drug habit is very expensive and more often than not drives young people into a life of crime,

with boys becoming thieves and pushers, and girls becoming prostitutes.

3. *Teenagers must dare to be different.* They must say a firm no to the use of drugs, including marijuana, whose dangers become more apparent with every new scientific study. Teenagers must not run away from the problems of life and try to find escape in drugs. They must face up to the deplorable conditions in society and work to improve them. They must be prudent in their choice of companions and the places they frequent, avoiding those which would lead them away from God anJ into trouble and sin. They should never take a drink or a cigarette from a stranger because some young people have become addicted in this way. They should bring their friends home with them to meet their parents, and should be encouraged by parents to consider the home as a place for wholesome social and recreational activities.

4. *The best preventive medicine against drug abuse is a solid family life and religious stability.* It is a fact that in homes where there is love and understanding and honest communication between parents and children, as well as family prayers and religious training, there is far less trouble with drug abuse than in homes where such an atmosphere does not exist. Parents and children who place their trust in God and ask for his divine assistance every day will be able to cope with whatever difficulties arise.

THE TEENAGER AND DRIVING

Teenagers are often blamed for evil deeds they do not do and for bad intentions they do not have. When such false accusations are hurled at young people, we come quickly to their defense. But there is one accusation that the strongest supporters of teenagers cannot refute; namely, that teenagers are a menace when they get behind the wheel of a car. This undeniable fact is reflected in the death and accident toll on the highways and in the higher insurance rates that teenagers must pay. Another indication is the dramatic increase in the number of fatal car accidents triggered by teenagers in states where the drinking age has been lowered.

The most aggravating thing about the bad driving record of teenagers is that they ought to be the best drivers on the road. The typical teenager is the one best equipped by nature to drive a car. Teenagers learn quickly, their senses are sharp and alert, their responses are fast, and they are able to perform mechanical functions with the greatest of ease. Since there is nothing wrong with their physical ability to drive, the problem must involve either their brains or their consciences.

As teenagers, perhaps all of us, or certainly some of us were blissfully unaware of the unbelievable number of teenager drivers who killed and injured people; blissfully unaware that there is a human limit to our ability to control a car; unaware of the ever-present possibility of a child running in front of our car, or some old lady unable to jump out of our way, or a man who is deaf who cannot hear our horn, or a little girl with poor vision who did not see us coming. Drop in at your local ambulance squad some day, or the fire and police rescue squads. They will be happy to see you, and willing to describe some of the accidents they saw. Or ask permission of your local hospital to spend a few minutes talking to the Emergency Room staff, who can tell you about arms ripped off, people blinded, people destroyed for life, people decapitated, children dying in the arms of their parents, and countless sad and sickening things, often caused by reckless driving. Once we realize that a car is a dangerous weapon, then it becomes a matter of conscience, a moral obligation, to drive carefully and at a safe and appropriate speed at all times.

Although more than 50,000 persons die in automobile accidents every year, teenagers — and many adults, too — do not seem to realize that the vehicle they are operating can be a lethal weapon. They engage in speeding, reckless driving, driving under the influence of alcohol or marijuana, using the car to vent anger and frustration, driving with utter disregard for traffic laws, and operating as if they owned the road. They offer convincing proof of the statement that it takes thousands of bolts to put a car together but only one nut to take it apart.

This kind of driving, whether they know it or not, is a sin. It is a violation of the fifth commandment, which forbids not only murder but also actions which could cause bodily harm. Perhaps Driver Education courses should include an explanation of the fifth commandment.

The moral implications of the automobile are not limited to the fifth commandment either. What about the sixth commandment, which forbids adultery, fornication, and other impure and unchaste acts? How many teenagers have violated this law of God in a car? How many illegitimate pregnancies, how many abortions, how many cases of venereal disease, how many heartaches and bitter disappointments, how many souls have been lost, all as a result of using the automobile as a "motel on wheels"?

Instead of an occasion of sin, your car can be a powerful means of building up Christian charity. How many times each day, especially in city driving, do we see opportunities to practice kindness toward pedestrians, meekness toward other drivers, patience in delay, tolerance of our brothers and sisters in Christ, long suffering toward habitual offenders, restraint and justice when we are tempted to blame an entire race or sex or ethnic group for the poor driving of one person?

You can even grow in holiness by being a good driver in the best sense of the term. Did you ever consider the possibility of engaging in group prayer while driving instead of spreading the latest gossip? Or suppose the next time someone cuts you off, instead of cursing him or making an obscene gesture or recklessly pursuing him, you say a prayer for the souls in purgatory? Imagine how many souls some of us would get to heaven in the course of a year!

The modern automobile is intended to serve mankind, not to destroy it. The proper use of a car offers a tremendous challenge to teenagers and their parents. They have a choice of death, destruction, financial woes, family troubles, loss of reputation, loss of purity — or possible growth in holiness. Which road do you choose?

YOUNG PEOPLE ARE IMPORTANT

The Second Vatican Council saw a great opportunity for young people to influence modern society. Citing their "zest for life and abounding energies to assume their own responsibility," as well as their yearning "to play their part in social and cultural life," the Council said that if this youthful zeal "is imbued with the spirit of Christ and is inspired by obedience to and love for the shepherds of the Church, it can be expected to be very fruitful. . . . In their own way, they can be true living witnesses to Christ among their companions" (*Decree on the Apostolate of the Laity*, No. 12).

In the same section of the document on the laity, the Council urged adults to "engage in friendly discussion with young people so that both groups, overcoming the age barrier, can become better acquainted and can share the special benefits each generation has to offer the other." Further, adults were told to attract young people to the apostolate by good example and "by offering them balanced advice and effectuve assistance." To the youth, the Council directed these words: "For their part, young people would be wise to cultivate toward adults respect and trust. Although the young are naturally attracted to new things, they should exercise an intelligent regard for worthwhile traditions."

The teenage years are difficult for parents and children. Those who have lived through the experience, however, assure us that teenagers eventually become people and, as parents, have just as much trouble understanding their own teenagers. If you think this situation is something new, consider the following remark:

I see no hope for the future of our people if they are dependent on the frivolous youth of today, for certainly all youth are reckless beyond words. . . . When I was a boy, we were taught to be discreet and respectful of elders.

These words come from a Greek writer of the Eighth Century before Christ.

*The apostolate of married persons
and of families is of unique
importance for the Church
and civil society.*
— Vatican Council II, *Decree on the
Apostolate of the Laity,* 11.

CHAPTER 7

Between
Family and Society

The family is the foundation of society. In it the various generations come together and help one another to grow wiser and to
harmonize personal rights with the other requirements of social
life. All those, therefore, who exercise influence over communities and social groups should work efficiently for the welfare of
marriage and the family. — Vatican II, *Pastoral Constitution on
the Church in the Modern World,* No. 52

When an architect draws up the blueprint for a building, he must carefully
avoid pitfalls or weak points in the plan lest the structure eventually come
tumbling down. Furthermore, the contractor must use good-quality materials in the construction of the building. Every now and then you read in
the newspapers about a building that collapsed, trapping or killing people
under the rubble. Usually, there is an investigation and sometimes a trial
at which those responsible for the faulty construction and planning are
convicted of negligence and either fined or sent to jail.

The family structure must also be based on a perfect blueprint (God's
divine plan) and must be built with good-quality materials (love, prayer,
work) if it is to stand tall and strong in our modern world. It must rest on
the foundation of God's moral law and teaching if it is to avoid the pitfalls
of selfishness and inordinate seeking of pleasure. And it must strive to resist
such weakening and destructive and false doctrines as contraception, sterilization, abortion, and euthanasia. If these moral termites are successful in
undermining the structure of the family, it will lead to the erosion and
collapse of our society just as surely as the widespread acceptance and tolerance of these illicit practices brought down earlier civilizations.

There is an anti-life climate in our land today. It has been brought
about by the actions of influential people in government, the news media,

and some members of the medical and scientific professions, and by the failure of Catholics and other people who look upon God as the Creator and absolute Ruler of all life to mount a united and vigorous campaign to protect innocent life from the moment of conception to natural death. The slogan of the anti-life forces is "quality of life," which means that some lives are of less value than others, that those who are deemed not to be capable of leading "a meaningful existence" should have their lives terminated, provided, of course, that they are allowed to come into existence at all.

There are many facets of the anti-life, and anti-family, climate: widespread voluntary use of birth control drugs and devices by individuals; the dissemination, by government, of contraceptives to dozens of nations around the world, as well as to countless welfare mothers and teenagers; increased "voluntary" sterilization of individuals; forced sterilization of welfare recipients, minors, and "mentally retarded or incompetent" persons; the killing of thousands of unborn babies every day by abortion; and putting people to death under the title of "euthanasia."

THE DIGNITY OF HUMAN LIFE

Before discussing the specific threat to the family posed by contraception, abortion, and euthanasia, let us review briefty the Catholic attitude regarding the dignity of human life. In the words of Vatican II:

Sacred Scripture teaches that man was created "to the image of God," is capable of knowing and loving his Creator, and was appointed by him as master of all earthly creatures that he might subdue them and use them to God's glory (*Pastoral Constitution on the Church in the Modern World*, No. 12).

God is the source of all human life and has created each one of us in his image and likeness as a unique individual. He has endowed each of us with certain abilities and talents, placed us on earth for a short period of time, and promised us eternal happiness if we do his will. Carrying out God's will involves using our abilities and talents to know, love, and serve him; to grow daily in holiness and perfection, and to act as an apostle and witness for him in the world.

The dignity of every person must be respected by other persons, by society, and by governments. God has shared his creative powers with his creatures and we must use those powers according to his divine plan. Governments, which are established to protect life, to sustain it when other means are lacking, and to guard the autonomy of the family, must never violate their solemn responsibilities. No matter what problems and difficulties may arise, said Pope John XXIII, "first place must be accorded every-thing that pertains to the dignity of man as such, or to the life of individual men, than which nothing can be more precious" (*Mater et Magistra*, No. 192).

CONTRACEPTION

There is a story told of a well-to-do and influential pagan Roman woman, Cornelia, who lived many centuries ago. On one occasion, she was entertaining a group of friends, attired in their finery and adorned with jewels. The group asked their hostess, "And now won't you show us your jewels?" Cornelia's answer was to call her children and introduce them: "These are my most precious jewels."

Those who favor the practice of birth prevention cite a number of reasons: financial difficulties, physical or emotional health, stability of the marriage, desire to give the fullest possible upbringing and education to al-ready existing children, and the dangers of unchecked population growth.

There is no question that there are some real hardship cases where the birth of a child could pose serious problems. But for many people prac-ticing birth control, let us be honest, the reasons given are not valid. The fi-nancial difficulties mentioned all too often mean not a denial of necessities but of luxuries; the emotional problems, which most parents experience at one time or another, are seldom insurmountable; the stability of the mar-riage cannot really be improved by undermining its holiness and rebelling against God; several children in a family does not mean sacrificing quality for quantity (consider how many famous people would never have been born if their parents had had only two children — Saint Ignatius, Saint Francis, Saint Catherine of Siena, Saint Therese, Father Jacques Mar-quette, John Paul Jones, Washington Irving, Sir Walter Scott, Alfred Lord Tennyson, Mozart, Wagner, Schubert, Pope John XXIII); and popula-tion projections into the future have been notoriously inaccurate.

Population growth can bring economic prosperity. The experience of the developing nations after World War II shows that high population growth was accompanied by high economic growth. At the World Popula-tion Conference in Bucharest in 1974, delegates from the developing na-tions of Africa and Latin America opposed attempts by the more developed and prosperous nations of the world to force birth control measures on them. A few weeks later, African Cardinal Maurice Otunga of Kenya told the Synod of Bishops in Rome that imposition of birth control on African countries as a condition for receiving economic aid was menacing their further development by disrupting the tradition of having large families. "Some governments have been assured of further aid on condition they accept family planning," the cardinal said. "It is a tragedy that such generosity has become such cruelty."*

The answer to population growth and starvation is social and economic development, not birth control and abortion. There is truth in the old saying: "Give a man a fish and he will eat for one day; teach him how to fish and he will eat for a lifetime." Half of the world's arable land, not to mention its oceans, has yet to be cultivated for food. Dr. Colin Clark, the widely respected economist and demographer, estimated that with the proper use of modern technology and agricultural methods, the earth could feed ten times its present population. It is a great paradox, Pope Paul told delegates to the World Food Conference in Rome in 1974, that people should go hungry at a time when man has "an unequaled mastery of the universe" and the "means capable of making the resources of the universe yield their full potential."

On the feast of Saint James the Apostle, July 25, 1968, Pope Paul VI issued an encyclical, "On Human Life," that restated the Catholic Church's centuries-old prohibition of artificial methods of birth control. Some people, led to believe that the Church was about to change a teaching that goes back to the earliest years of Christianity, expressed surprise and shock. They should not have been either surprised or shocked, for there are few teachings of the Church that have been reaffirmed more often than the teaching on the proper regulation of birth. Just in recent decades, for example, artificial contraception has been condemned by Pope Pius XI (1930), Pope Pius XII (1951 and 1958), Pope John XXIII (1961), the Second Vatican Council (1965), and Pope Paul VI (1964, 1965, and 1966). After *Humanae Vitae* was promulgated, the Holy Father reiterated the Church's teaching on birth control several more times, leaving, one would think, no doubt in anyone's mind where the Church stands on this issue.

Humanae Vitae has been criticized as a negative document written by a bachelor Pope who had little or no idea about the problems faced by married couples and society at large. It has been dismissed as the non-infallible opinion of one man, with whom Catholics are free to agree or disagree. It has been rejected as a not very scholarly or intellectual treatment

*Peter J. Shaw, United Press International, October 3, 1974.

of a matter that could be much better handled by certain "theologians." Are these criticisms valid? They are not valid.

The truth is that *Humanae Vitae* is a profound treatment of life and love; a proclamation of the positive values of love, marriage, parenthood, and family; a consistent, authoritative, and morally binding statement by the Vicar of Christ, and, in the words of Cardinal John J. Wright, "a prophetic defense of man, of the human person, and of the future of the race."*

The encyclical defends human sexuality against mere sex, declares that the life-giving and love-giving aspects of marital intercourse cannot be separated, and reminds Christian married couples that the strength they need to observe this difficult teaching can be found in prayer and the sacraments.

To those who contend that Catholics do not have an obligation to follow this teaching because the Pope was not speaking *ex cathedra*, that is, from the chair of Peter, or infallibly, we call to their attention the words of Vatican II:

> In matters of faith and morals, the bishops speak in the name of Christ and the faithful are to accept their teaching and adhere to it with a religious assent of soul. This religious submission of will and of mind must be shown in a special way to the authentic teaching authority of the Roman Pontiff, even when he is not speaking *ex cathedra*. That is, it must be shown in such a way that his supreme magisterium is acknowledged with reverence, the judgments made by him are sincerely adhered to, according to his manifest mind and will. His mind and will in the matter may be known chiefly either from the character of the documents, from his frequent repetition of the same doctrine, or from his manner of speaking (*Dogmatic Constitution on the Church*, No. 25).

The Pope, either alone or in conjunction with the bishops of the world, is the only authoritative teacher and authentic interpreter of the law of God. No theologian, priest, sister, brother, or layperson — whatever their sincerity, popularity, or academic or professional credentials — can be followed if they teach a doctrine contrary to the official and authoritative

*Cardinal John J. Wright, "Reflections on a Controverted Encyclical," *Friar*, November 1971, p. 9.

teaching of the Holy Father. The teachings of those who contradict the authentic interpretations of the Vicar of Christ must be rejected.

WHY IS CONTRACEPTION WRONG?

Contraception is any direct, positive frustration of any phase in the process of conception before, during, or after a voluntary act of intercourse. It is the clear, unmistakable, and unchanging teaching of the Catholic Church that contraception is always and everywhere evil, immoral, and sinful. The use of contraceptives of whatever type and for however long a time can never be objectively condoned or justified as a morally acceptable means of controlling births or limiting the size of a family.

Please note that we are talking strictly about the evil of contraception itself, not about the guilt of persons who practice it. This important distinction can be illustrated by recalling the three conditions for mortal sin — grave matter, sufficient reflection, and full consent of the will. We are saying only that the practice of birth control is grave matter. Whether couples fully meet the other two conditions, or whether their moral guilt is reduced by ignorance or weakness, are matters that only God can judge.

The evils of contraception are not confined to the violation of the divine and natural law and the refusal of a couple to join with God in the creation of a new life. Birth control, as Pope Paul said in *Humanae Vitae* (No. 17), is also destructive of the person and disastrous to society. It brings to a marriage selfishness, infidelity, lack of self-sacrifice, and the loss of respect for the woman, who is treated as a thing to be used and not as a person to be loved and respected. Would any husband who truly loved his wife allow her to risk her health and even her life by taking contraceptive medication or using some intrauterine device? Mahatma Gandhi, the great Hindu leader, was right when he said in 1946: "Contraceptives are an insult to womanhood. The difference between a prostitute and a woman using contraceptives is only that the former sells her body to several men, the latter sells it to one man."*

Contraception is also disastrous to society, bringing about a general lowering of morality, placing a dangerous weapon in the hands of government, and paving the way for abortion and euthanasia. Who would deny

*Quoted by Charles E. Rice, *Authority and Rebellion*, Garden City, New York: Doubleday & Company, 1971, p. 30.

that these grave consequences have come about since they were forecast by Pope Paul in *Humanae Vitae?* Each year that passes confirms the wisdom and foresight of the Holy Father and the absolute necessity of rejecting the contraceptive mentality and returning to the true Christian concept of married life and love.

RESPONSIBLE PARENTHOOD

At this point, the question naturally arises: How many children is a married couple expected to have? Does the Church's teaching mean that a woman has to have a baby every year? What is the Church's position on family size and responsible parenthood?

Married couples are expected to "be ready with stout hearts" to cooperate with God in bringing children into the world. This does not mean that couples must have an unlimited number of children; that they cannot have reasonable intervals between births; that they cannot take into account the harmony and peace of the family, and the welfare and education of the children they already have.

Responsible parenthood, according to the Second Vatican Council, means that couples "thoughtfully take into account both their own welfare and that of their children, those already born and those which may be foreseen. For this accounting they will reckon with both the material and the spiritual conditions of the times as well as of their state in life. Finally, they will consult the interests of the family group, of temporal society, and of the Church herself" (*Pastoral Constitution on the Church in the Modern World*, No. 50).

However, in the same paragraph, the Council went on to say that "the parents themselves should ultimately make this judgment in the sight of God. But in their manner of acting, spouses should be aware that they cannot proceed arbitrarily. They must always be governed according to a conscience dutifully conformed to the divine law itself, and should be submissive toward the Church's teaching office, which authentically interprets that law in the light of the Gospel."

Clarifying this point further, the Council also said that in "harmonizing conjugal love with the responsible transmission of life . . . sons of the Church may not undertake methods of regulating procreation which are found blameworthy by the teaching authority of the Church in its unfolding of the divine law" (*Pastoral Constitution on the Church in the Modern World*, No. 51).

In other words, the practice of responsible parenthood cannot involve the use of artificial methods of birth control, or sterilization, or abortion to limit the size of a family. The firm teaching of the Church is that "each and every marriage act must remain open to the transmission of life" (*Humanae Vitae,* No. 11). For those couples who have "serious motives to space out births," Pope Paul said in his encyclical, their only recourse is the method known as rhythm, which means abstaining from marital relations during those days when a woman is fertile and capable of conceiving a child.

The problem with rhythm has been to pinpoint exactly the fertile days. The old calendar method was not very reliable. Today, however, new methods have been developed and advocates of natural family planning insist that these methods are safer than chemical means and more effective than mechanical means. Couples seeking information on natural methods should contact the Family Life Bureau in their diocese.

Rhythm involves a willingness to restrain one's sexual impulses, a suggestion that is not very popular in a society that frowns on any kind of self-control. But there are definite advantages to this method, including the fact that it requires the cooperation of both parties, as opposed to other methods which place the burden of responsibility on one partner. This mutual involvement of husband and wife, which will demand real communication between them, can enhance the respect, increase the affection, and deepen the love which they feel for each other.

The Church's teaching on responsible parenthood is a hard teaching, but millions of couples have tried and are trying to follow it. There are some who do not always succeed and to them Pope Paul offers this compassionate advice: "Let them implore divine assistance by persevering prayer; above all, let them draw from the source of grace and charity in the Eucharist. And if sin should still keep its hold over them, let them not be discouraged, but rather have recourse with humble perseverance to the mercy of God, which is poured forth in the sacrament of Penance" (*Humanae Vitae,* No. 25).

Vatican II also had a word of praise for those couples who choose to have large families, saying that they "merit special mention who with wise and common deliberation, and with a gallant heart, undertake to bring up suitably even a relatively large family" (*Pastoral Constitution on the Church in the Modern World,* No. 50). These couples do indeed have gallant hearts and can identify with the following humorous, but very true, observation made by entertainer Victor Borge: "People sometimes ask me if I think of myself first as a musician or a comedian. I never think of myself first — not with five children."

When Cardinal Eugenio Pacelli, who later became Pope Pius XII, was traveling to Argentina for the Eucharistic Congress of 1934, a little child came up to him and playfully removed the Cardinal's pectoral cross and chain and placed it around his own neck. The father of the child rushed forward and scolded him. "Don't scold him," Cardinal Pacelli said, "I lent him the cross because little children bless everything they touch." This remark of the man who was soon to become Pope reflects the attitude of Christ himself, who once told the Apostles: "Let the children come to me and do not hinder them. It is to just such as these that the kingdom of God belongs" (Mk. 10:14). And on another occasion, our Lord said: "Whoever welcomes a child such as this for my sake welcomes me" (Mk. 9:37).

ABORTION

Abortion is the expulsion of a non-viable fetus. We are not talking about spontaneous abortion, popularly known as miscarriage, which often results from disease or accident or some unknown cause; nor about indirect abortion, which results from a medical procedure to preserve the life or health of the mother, such as the removal of a cancerous uterus. We are referring to the killing of a developing baby for social, economic, or other reasons, primarily the convenience of the mother.

The scope of abortion very nearly defies comprehension. In the year following the infamous "Black Monday" decision of the United States Supreme Court on January 22, 1973, an estimated 1.5 million unborn babies were deprived of their God-given right to life in the United States. This death toll is greater than all the American deaths in all the wars in our 200-year history.

WHEN DOES HUMAN LIFE BEGIN?

For many people, the word abortion does not have much significance because they are not aware of when human life begins or of how the child develops in the mother's womb. They have been misled by the false and misleading terminology used by the death peddlers. Instead of saying unborn child, they say "glob of protoplasm." Instead of a human being with potential, they say "potential human." Instead of killing an unborn baby, they say "termination of pregnancy."

In October 1967, a distinguished group of experts in the fields of medicine, law, ethics, and the social sciences met in Washington, D.C., for the

First International Conference on Abortion. Asked to consider the question of when human life begins, the almost unanimous conclusion (19 to 1) of the group was as follows:

> The majority of the group could find no point in time between the union of sperm and egg, or at least the blastocyst stage, and the birth of the infant at which point we could say that this was not a human life. [The blastocyst stage occurs shortly after fertilization.] The changes occurring between implantation, a six-weeks embryo, a six-months fetus, a one-week child, or a mature adult are merely stages of development and maturation.*

Modern science has provided us with a clear description of human life from the moment of conception, when the sperm cell from the father fertilizes the egg cell from the mother. Each parent contributes 23 chromosomes to the fertilized ovum, which now becomes a unique being with its own genetic package that has already determined its future height, the color of its eyes, and other characteristics. The development of the unborn child takes place as follows:

1.   The fertilized egg is implanted in the wall of the uterus seven to nine days after conception.

2.   Blood cells are present seventeen days after fertilization.

3.   The heart begins to beat at eighteen days.

4.   The foundation of the brain, spinal cord, and nervous system is established by the twentieth day.

5.   At thirty days, the unborn child is a quarter of an inch long, is made up of millions of cells and, under a powerful microscope, looks human. The baby is now 10,000 times larger than the original fertilized ovum.

6.   Measurable brain waves can be recorded by the forty-third day, a sure sign that life is present. The child begins to move at this point, although it will be another fourteen weeks or so before the mother feels any life.

7.   By the eighth week, every body system of the child is present, and all of them will be working by the eleventh week. During this period of time, the child becomes very active, kicking his legs, sucking his thumb, turning his head, squinting and frowning, drinking the amniotic fluid that surrounds him — more if the fluid is sweetened and less if it has a sour taste.

*cf. Dr. and Mrs. J. C. Willke, *Handbook on Abortion,* Cincinnati, Ohio: Hiltz Publishing Company, 1973, p. 8.

8.   The child weighs about one ounce at twelve weeks after fertilization and can feel pain. Unborn children have been known to push away or grasp instruments or needles inserted into the uterus.

9.   The child grows rapidly during the next few weeks, reaching a weight of one pound and a height of one foot by the twentieth week. About ten per cent of babies born between twenty and twenty-four weeks gestation will survive, even though they are just past the halfway point in the pregnancy.

10.   If no attempt is made to kill the unborn child, he will grow in size and strength over the next three or four months and will enter the world.

GET RID OF THE PROBLEM, NOT THE BABY

How anyone who knows these facts of fetal development, especially the mother, who should be the natural protectress of her own child, can inflict violent death on these modern-day Holy Innocents to solve personal or social problems is difficult to perceive. The methods of abortion are cruel and barbaric whether they involve cutting, scraping, or vacuuming the child from the wall of the uterus, burning the child to death with a salt solution, or removing the child alive and then tossing him or her into a bucket to die. It is difficult not to use the term murder when discussing the fate of these little ones.

The reasons given to justify this legalized slaughter of the unborn, while plausible sounding on the surface, have no validity when subjected to careful scrutiny. The reasons include the physical or mental health of the mother, pregnancy resulting from rape or incest, the child will not be wanted, the "population explosion," the possibility of a deformed child, the need to reduce the number of illegal abortions, and a woman's "right" to control her own body.

In point of fact, modern-day advances in medicine have eliminated practically every medical indication for abortion. There is no physical problem or ailment that cannot be treated while a women is pregnant. Doctors never really have to decide whether to save the life of the mother or the baby; they do everything possible to save the lives of both their patients. As for the mental health of the mother, there is no known psychiatric ailment that can be cured by abortion. If a woman has a mental problem, she can be treated during and after the pregnancy. And it should be noted that not a few women have developed mental problems *as a result* of abortion. The mental health excuse is used to justify most abortions but it really means that a woman is looking for a convenient way to get rid of her baby.

Pregnancy resulting from rape or incest is so rare as to be almost non-existent. But even if such a pregnancy should occur, is abortion the answer? Will killing the child remove the emotional scar left by the rape, or will it add another emotional scar? And what kind of logic is it that would punish the child for the sin of his father? Furthermore, the incidence of sterility among women, particularly teenagers, having abortions is noteworthy. Would it not be better to carry the child to full term and put him up for adoption rather than risk sterility and the possibility of never being able to have another child?

Many unwanted pregnancies result in the course of time in truly wanted children. But if a woman does not want to keep her baby, she can put him up for adoption. The number of couples desiring to adopt a child exceeds the number of children available. Nor does abortion eliminate the problem of the battered child. A study in California some years ago of 400 battered children showed that ninety per cent of them were wanted by their parents. The "population explosion" problem we have already discussed in connection with birth control.

The possibility of a deformed child, while a hardship on parents, still cannot justify killing the child. Many retarded or handicapped children can lead reasonably normal lives and the love and affection shown to these children by their parents is a joy to behold. Permitting the killing of unborn children who might be defective is a dangerous step because it would lead to the killing of any defective human being, regardless of age. A more humane approach to this problem would be to encourage continued research into birth defects, improve treatment of deformed children, and provide supportive measures for families raising children with such problems.

What must we say of the need to reduce the number of *illegal* abortions? By following this channel of social reform, we could do away with all crime by doing away with all laws. In point of fact, we cannot divorce this social problem from the realm of morality by relegating it exclusively to the sphere of legality.

A relatively new reason for abortion involves the "right" of a woman to control her own body. The time for a woman to control her own body is before she becomes pregnant. Once she is pregnant, there is a third party involved — the unborn child. This baby is not a part of her body, but has its own completely separate humanity. Any discussion of rights must include the baby's rights. And speaking to the so-called "right of privacy" which the Supreme Court said allows a woman to kill her unborn child anytime in the first three months without state interference, may we suggest that even if such a "right of privacy" did exist in the Constitution of the United States, it would not supersede the right to life which is our most basic right and without which none of our other rights would have any meaning.

All of this is not to deny that pregnancy does pose serious problems for some women. However, the right to life and to birth must always be protected. The answer, therefore, is to get rid of the problem, not the baby. If a woman is contemplating abortion because of seemingly desperate difficulties, she deserves positive, humane assistance to solve her problems. Fortunately, there are organizations which are providing an alternative to abortion: encouragement to have the baby, help in finding the medical and financial assistance to do so, and counselling and a sympathetic ear during and after the pregnancy. Here is a real opportunity to practice Christian charity. Will you accept the challenge?

Abortion is not a Catholic issue, although the Church has condemned the killing of unborn children as an "unspeakable crime" (Vatican II, *Pastoral Constitution on the Church in the Modern World*, No. 51), imposed excommunication on any Catholic who participates in an abortion with full knowledge of the Church's penalty (U.S. Bishops' Pastoral Letter on Abortion, February 13, 1973), and declared that "a Christian can never conform to a law that makes abortion legal" (Vatican Congregation for the Doctrine of the Faith, *Declaration on Procured Abortion*, November 18, 1974, No. 22). Abortion is a human issue and should be rejected by every person who values his or her humanity, regardless of religious beliefs. Failure to act on behalf of the innocent, helpless, defenseless, voiceless unborn is inexcusable, immoral, and a repudiation of the teaching of Christ: "As often as you did it for one of my least brothers, you did it for me" (Mt. 25:40).

EUTHANASIA

A woman who had grown tired of caring for her old and sick mother decided to get rid of her. She called her son and told him to put his grandmother in the wagon and take her out in the woods and leave her there to die. She also told him to leave the wagon with the grandmother. The young man did as he was told except that when he returned a few hours later, he had brought the wagon back with him. When his mother asked why, he replied: "Someday you will be old and sick and I'll need the wagon to take you out in the woods to die."

Since human life is a continuum from the moment of conception to the moment of death, it is logical, if one believes in killing the child in the womb by abortion, to argue that the life of a born person — infant, child, adolescent, adult, or senior citizen — can also be terminated. Either all life is sacred or no life is sacred. Those who tolerated or approved contraception got abortion. Those who tolerate or approve abortion will get euthanasia. They may get it personally if some "quality of life" enforcer decides that they are not leading "a meaningful existence," which means that they have become a social or economic, or perhaps political or religious, burden to someone. Adults may find themselves faced with three choices: be nice to their children, get on the committee that decides who shall live and who shall die, or fight the mercy killers.

Euthanasia is the direct killing of those who, while they have committed no crime deserving of death, are because of mental or physical defects considered of no further value to society. We are told that the killing is being done for the good of the patient. In fact, euthanasia is not uncommonly done for the convenience of the family, or the hospital or institution, or society.

DEATH WITH DIGNITY OR MURDER?

Many people are strongly opposed to taking the life of even a person with a terminal illness. So the promoters of euthanasia coined the slogan "death with dignity" to soften the implications of what they are doing and to deceive the unwary. Now who does not want to die with dignity? But what do the mercy killers mean by this phrase? They mean to bring about the death of a person so that he or she will no longer be a burden to others, will no longer interfere with the comfort and convenience of family or relatives, will no longer take up space in a hospital or institution that could be better utilized by someone else, and will no longer "waste" funds on care and therapy that could be better spent for more positive and constructive programs.

The Christian looks at "death with dignity" in a different light. In the words of Cardinal Humberto Medeiros of Boston: "I interpret 'death with dignity' as the sick person being with family, relatives, and loved ones; receiving excellent medical and nursing care in an attractive environment; obtaining the ordinary means of sustaining life and extraordinary means if they choose, and surrounded by the priest or clergyman who provides religious and spiritual consolation."*

The distinction between ordinary and extraordinary means is important. To preserve life we must take ordinary means, but usually we need not take extraordinary means. Some things are quite clearly in most circumstances ordinary, such as the taking of some medicine, or a minor operation on one's foot. Others are quite clearly extraordinary, such as the amputation of two legs. Traditional Catholic belief was long ago succinctly proclaimed to the world by Pope Pius XII:

> Natural reason and Christian morality say that man (and whoever is entrusted with the task of taking care of his fellow-man) has the right and the duty in case of serious illness to employ the measures necessary for the preservation of life and health. Normally one is held only to use ordinary means — according to circumstances of persons, places, times and culture, — that is to say, means that do not involve any grave burden for oneself or another. On the other hand, man is not forbidden to take more than the strictly necessary steps to preserve life and health.
>
> The rights and duties of the doctor are correlative to those of the patient. The doctor, in fact, has no separate or independent right where the patient is concerned. In general he can take action only if the patient explicitly or implicitly, directly or indirectly, gives him permission. The rights and duties of the family generally depend upon the presumed will of the unconscious patient. Where the proper and independent duty of the family is concerned, they are usually bound only to the use of ordinary means . . .
>
> All forms of direct euthanasia, that is the administration of a drug in order to produce or hasten death, are unlawful, because in that case one asserts the right to dispose directly of life.**

The time has come to reject the legalization of euthanasia, "death with dignity" statutes, "living wills" which sanction euthanasia, not only because they are immoral, but also because they are unnecessary. The principle concerning ordinary and extraordinary means is the moral and sound medical course of action for the seriously ill and dying. It also leaves room for the Christian concept of redemptive suffering, which, experience

*Cardinal Humberto Medeiros, Homily at a Special Liturgy for Life, December 28, 1974.
**Address of Pope Pius XII, February 14, 1957. Extracts.

has shown, often brings out the finest qualities in people, both the person who is suffering and those who show love for him by caring for him.

THE LIFE YOU SAVE MAY BE YOUR OWN

The attack on innocent human life, and on the family structure, has reached frightening proportions today. While many people might not have been affected by contraception and abortion, all are potential victims of the mercy killers. No longer can you hide your head in the sand and say that you do not want to get involved. You are involved. And this time the life you save could be your own.

The Christian call to action has never been clearer. Cardinal Medeiros gave the challenge:

We must convince society that God has authority and dominion over life; that as he alone created human life, he alone can terminate it; that every person, however ill, disadvantaged, impaired, handicapped, or aged, can still fulfill the divine purpose of creation which is for us to know, love, serve, praise, worship and give glory to God; to grow in goodness, virtue, and perfection; to advance towards sainthood — and therefore to be loved by the Creator. This is to live a meaningful life and, in God's good time, all of us can and should die with dignity.*

*Cardinal Humberto Medeiros, Homily at a Special Liturgy for Life, December 28, 1974.

CHAPTER 8

Between Family and God

Married couples and Christian parents should follow their own proper path to holiness by faithful love, sustaining one another in grace throughout the entire length of their lives. They should imbue their offspring, lovingly welcomed from God, with Christian truths and evangelical virtues. For thus they can offer all men an example of unwearying and generous love, build up the brotherhood of charity, and stand as witnesses to and cooperators in the fruitfulness of Holy Mother Church. — Vatican II, *Dogmatic Constitution on the Church*, No. 41

On the wall of the Research Department of a large industrial firm, one visitor was surprised to see this sign in a prominent place: "The problem when solved will be simple."

We might apply those words to the present-day state of marriage and the family. Yes, there are many problems today eating away at the very foundations of the family. But the solution to those problems is not difficult; it is simply a return to Christ's blueprint of family life. God is the author of marriage and the family, and if we are wise, we will look to him for the design of the ideal family.

Today the spirit of paganism, hedonism, and selfishness has made serious inroads in the field of marriage. Sometimes it is due to ignorance, sometimes to malice. Christ's very explicit norms and ideals are being ignored and scoffed at on a widespread scale. Divorce, birth control, marital infidelity and unhappiness, abortion, euthanasia, rejection of the divine origin of marriage — all these elements are much too evident in our twentieth century society.

FOLLOW THE INSTRUCTIONS

Whenever things deviate from their right order, as marriage and the

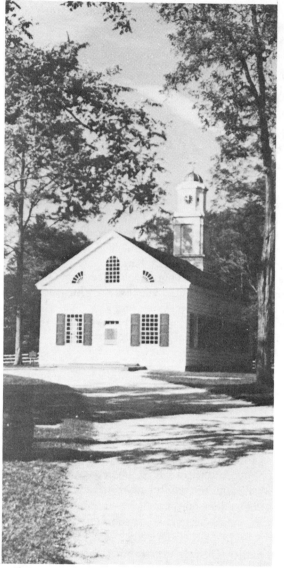

*Blest are they
who hunger and thirst
for holiness.*
— (Mt. 5:6).

family have done, difficulties will arise. When the manufacturer of an automobile gives a set of instructions with it, the wise thing is to obey the directions; he who will not do so causes trouble for himself. When God instituted the family, he gave a set of instructions to be obeyed. When the world cast them aside, problems began to occur. The basic answer to these problems today is a return to the divine plan.

God has laid down basic norms upon which the home must be based and our lives must be lived. Following these norms requires sacrifice and generosity. Families should try to carry out God's will and not their own, because his way is the only sure way to true happiness. God blessed the first marriage in the Garden of Eden. God is the author and partner of every marriage today. If that fact were more widely acknowledged and accepted, families would be happier.

HELP FROM GOD'S CHURCH

Families must know Christ's teachings in order to follow them. Back in 1930, Pope Pius XI, in his encyclical on Christian marriage, warned the world that the "subverters of marriage are entirely devoted to misleading the minds of men and corrupting their hearts, to making a mockery of matrimonial purity and extolling the filthiest of vices by means of books and pamphlets and other innumerable methods." The Holy Father said that we should, "by every fitting means, oppose error by truth, vice by the excellent dignity of chastity, the slavery of covetousness by the liberty of the sons of God, that disastrous ease in obtaining divorce by an enduring love in the bond of marriage and by the inviolate pledge of fidelity given even to death" (*Casti Connubii*, No. 106).

Four decades later, Pope Paul VI echoed his predecessor in the pontificate, saying that the Church's teaching on married life "will perhaps not be easily received by all. Too numerous are those voices amplified by the modern means of propaganda, which are contrary to the voice of the Church" (*Humanae Vitae*, No. 18). And like Pius XI, Pope Paul emphasized how "great indeed is the work of education, of progress, and of love to which we call you. . . . Truly a great work . . . since man cannot find true happiness . . . other than in respect of the laws written by God in his very nature, laws which he must observe with intelligence and love" (*Humanae Vitae*, No. 31).

The truth that we need to fight the "subverters of marriage" can be found in the consistent and coherent teaching of the Church over the centuries, particularly since 1930. Those seeking sound instruction on marriage and the family should consult the encyclicals *Casti Conubii* and *Humanae Vitae* and the documents of the Second Vatican Council, especially Sections 47-52 of the *Pastoral Constitution on the Church in the Modern World.*

If there is to be an effective restoration of the divine plan with regard to the family, then the divine laws of marriage must be known with certainty and applied to our times. There must be an authoritative guide. That guide is the Holy Father, the successor of Saint Peter, whom Christ himself commissioned to teach all nations "to carry out everything I have commanded you" and to whom Christ promised to be "with you always, until the end of the world" (Mt. 28:20). The Pope and the bishops are responsible for guarding and interpreting the moral law handed to them by Christ and they deserve our wholehearted cooperation and obedience.

Those families who are trying to live up to the ideals of family life urged by Christ and the Catholic Church help not only themselves but act as a beacon of light to all those around them. Good, as well as bad, can spread like contagion or infection. One ideal family can have an influence it might never suspect. Such families must let their light shine before the world.

THE IDEAL FAMILY

You recall the occasion when Christ was anointed with precious ointment and the question was asked: "What is the point of this extravagant waste?" (Mk. 14:4). The same question has also been asked about the life of the Holy Family at Nazareth. Why did Christ spend thirty years of his life with Mary and Joseph, accomplishing apparently so little? Why did Christ, who came into this world on so sublime and important a mission, spend thirty years in just ordinary living? Why this waste?

It was through thirty hidden years that Christ sanctified and gave new meaning to "ordinary" family life. He spent these years with Mary and Joseph to teach the world the lesson of the importance of family life, of the sanctity of the home, that "ordinary" lives are enough if modeled on the Holy Family. Nazareth was meant to teach the world an important lesson.

If we could have observed that home two thousand years ago, we would have noticed Jesus, liked by the people in the town, obedient and devoted to his family. We would have seen Mary going about her tasks, going to the town well to draw water as was the woman's duty. We would have noticed Mary as a woman devoted to her duty as a mother, quick to help anyone in trouble, self-sacrificing. We would have noticed her modesty in dress and manner and would have sensed her strong character and virtue. We would have seen that the underlying motive of her life was complete submission to God's will in even the smallest events of her life, a principle of life expressed in her own words: "Let it be done to me as you say" (Lk. 1:38).

We would have noticed Joseph as a man who knew his trade, did his job well, and was not only satisfied but happy to be with his family when his work was done. In Joseph we have a concrete example of the new meaning which has been given to the dignity of labor. All of us cannot imitate the example of the saints who were great apostles or scholars or who devoted their entire lives to the care of the poor or sick. But the example of Joseph, the head of a family, is within reach of all. He worked no miracles that we know of; he did nothing outstanding. But what he did, he did wholeheartedly for Christ.

Jesus attached great importance to just "ordinary" family life. He spent thirty years in such an environment. Nazareth is a concrete example of how the modern family might return to Christ's ideal of family life. Christ should be the head of every family, the witness of every deed, the reader of every thought. The family should speak to him daily in prayer. How can selfishness, or anger, or strife, or impurity, or drunkenness enter a household wherein there is a keen realization of Christ's presence? The home of the Holy Family at Nazareth is the ideal to which all Christian families should aspire.

FOUR BONDS OF FAMILY LIFE

Four strong bonds have traditionally held families together: the bond of affection, the bond of common work, the bond of common prayer, and the bond of common play. An observer of the modern family could not help but notice that these bonds, particularly the last three, have been greatly weakened. The bond of affection of itself is not enough to keep a family stable. There must be something more. The restoration of the family might well come about sooner than we expect if more families would work together, pray together, and play together.

THE BOND OF AFFECTION

We have already discussed love and affection as essential ingredients in any Christian family, but we might recapitulate. The family is the school of love, a manifestation of the love of God for his Church and for us. Any family who shuts out Christ shuts out love. In the book of Revelation,

Christ says: "Here I stand, knocking at the door. If anyone hears me calling and opens the door, I will enter his house and have supper with him, and he with me" (Rv. 3:20). Christian families who open the door to Christ will have him in their homes just as he was in the home of Martha and Mary.

Children learn of love early in life when mother or dad tucks them in at night, takes care of them when they are sick, gives them birthday parties, and cares for them in a thousand ways. This is the time to tell children that God loves them in the same way. Children who are really loved will respond with real love. In observing and sharing affection, kindness, and concern for others, the love of a family continues to grow and is a beautiful sight to behold. A happy and loving family is a foretaste of heaven.

THE BOND OF WORK

A family should be like the oarsmen in a boat, with each member doing his or her share to keep the family functioning efficiently and smoothly. No one likes to do chores, but they are an unavoidable part of life and can be made less irksome if everyone pitches in. Parents should make chores a cooperative exercise so as to eliminate the drudgery. They should explain to the children about the operation and expense of maintaining a home and family and the consequent need for everyone's cooperation and assistance. Keeping the house and property clean, comfortable, and cozy should be the goal of every family. If all contribute enthusiastically to the realization of this goal, they will experience the satisfaction of a job well done and will be bound closer together.

Here are some tips for parents with regard to family chores and responsibilities:

1.   Children can be paid allowances, but they should not be bribed to do chores. They must understand that chores are a normal and expected contribution to the well-being of the family.

2.   Work well done should be praised. We all need encouragement and praise, especially when we have completed a task we would rather not have tackled in the first place. Frequent praise will inspire enthusiasm and a willingness to perform chores in the future.

3.   Parents should not always insist on having chores done exactly as they would do them. Give children some flexibility.

4.   When chores are completed, let the children go about their own activities. Children who are still restricted after chores are done will come to resent even minor tasks and minimal demands on their time.

5. Parents should watch their own attitudes toward household duties and responsibilities. If they treat a job as unpleasant, so will the children. But if parents undertake projects cheerfully, they will encourage a similar attitude in the children.

THE BOND OF PRAYER

In years gone by, and among various religions, prayer was considered as essential in the home as in church. Morning and evening prayers in common were the rule. In one period of Protestantism, the family regularly assembled for family prayer, led by the father of the house. Family prayer played and still plays an important part in the Orthodox Jewish tradition. The family rosary must be marked down as a potent factor in the preservation of Catholic faith and Catholic family life.

Today, however, there is less emphasis on family prayer, which may explain in part the increasing break-up of families, as well as the tense and even hostile atmosphere that exists in some families. The time has come for a return to family prayer, for a restating of the slogan, "The family that prays together stays together."

The Morning Offering, grace at meals, consecration of the family to the Sacred Heart, the family rosary, Bible reading, and night prayers in common are all powerful means of drawing the family closer together. From the very outset of their marriage, a husband and wife should make a practice of reciting their prayers in common. Any difficulties that may spring up in the course of the day will then tend to disappear. How can ill feeling or a grudge last for long with one who is praying by your side?

The important contribution that prayerful parents can make to their family life was once summed up by General Douglas MacArthur:

By profession I am a soldier and take pride in that fact, but I am prouder, infinitely prouder, to be a father. A soldier destroys in order to build; the father only builds, never destroys. The one has the potentialities of death; the other embodies creation and life. And, while the hordes of death are mighty, the battalions of life are mightier still. It is my hope that my son, when I am gone, will remember me not for the battle but in the home repeating with him our simple daily prayer, "Our Father who art in heaven."

Family prayer does not have to be restricted to a definite time every night, with every member of the house present under pain of excommunication. It can be flexible; it can be held at different times to accommodate family members who have other obligations; it can even be said with some members missing for good reasons. The important thing is that the family should pray together often. Common prayer can not only bring peace to troubled homes and be a means of solving difficulties, but also can solidify the foundation on which true Christian families are built. In the words of the Second Vatican Council:

> With their parents leading the way by example and family prayer, children and indeed everyone gathered around the family hearth will find a readier path to human maturity, salvation, and holiness. (*Pastoral Constitution on the Church in the Modern World*, No. 48).

Another important feature of a Catholic home is the presence of religious articles and books, such as crucifixes, statues of Jesus and the Blessed Mother (perhaps even a shrine in your yard), holy pictures, a Bible, a sick-call set for emergencies, a bottle of holy water, Catholic periodicals and other literature. All of these are reminders of God's presence in our homes and in our lives. How can we expect children to grow up with a knowledge and love of Christ and his mother if their only exposure to their religion is one hour a week in a church building?

Is your home a Catholic home? Do Jesus and Mary have an important place in your family? Consider the following checklist and decide:

Are morning and night prayers a daily occurrence in your home?

Do you say grace before and thanks to God after meals?

Do you say a family rosary every night?

Do you carry a rosary at all times?

Do you wear a religious medal or a scapular?

Do you read and discuss the Bible often?

Is your home dedicated to the Sacred Heart of Jesus?

Is there a cross hanging in a prominent place?

Do you ask God's help in the solution of family problems?

Do you have a sick-call set for Communion or anointing of the sick?

Do you attend church as a family?

Do you go to confession regularly?

Do the children attend a Catholic school or religious instruction program?

Do you have religious instruction at home?

Are there Catholic periodicals in your home?

Do you have a crib at Christmas?

Do you send out Christmas cards that indicate that Christmas is the birth of Christ?

Does it mean the coming of Christ or a chance to get gifts?

Does Easter Sunday mean the resurrection of Christ or new clothes?

Do you ever invite lonesome or needy people to your home?

Do you ever provide a basket of food to a needy family, not just at Thanksgiving and Christmas but during the year?

In the lounge of a certain nurses' home in a Catholic hospital, there is an arm chair with a silken cord tied across the arms. It is called "The Master's Chair," and represents the presence of Jesus in the home. It is a constant reminder that Christ has a place in the life of every nurse. That should be the spirit of every Christian home: The Master's Chair. Christ has a place. His presence is acknowledged.

In the famous painting of Christ knocking at the door, there is no handle to be seen. It is said that the artist made this omission purposely, because Christ never forces his way in; he must be admitted by those inside. Is it possible that the Savior has been waiting outside your door all this time? Like the innkeeper of long ago, have you refused admission to Mary and Joseph? If so, you and your children have suffered a great loss.

Bring Jesus and Mary and Joseph into your home today. Once you really get to know them, you and your family will love them. And with that love will come the greatest happiness and confidence. All the temptations of modern life will hold no fear for you and your family, because your help is in the name of the Lord, who made heaven and earth. The same Lord who promised that "where two or three are gathered in my name, there am I in their midst" (Mt. 18:20), will shower his blessings on your home.

THE BOND OF PLAY

One of the important tasks which faces families today is the restoration of family play or recreation. Families have almost lost the ability to enjoy each other. Dad goes off to one activity, mother to another, and the children to their pursuits. Thus, the family misses out on an opportunity to learn to enjoy and understand each other. Another obstacle is put in the way of family togetherness. What can be done to improve this situation?

First, we must get an idea of what recreation means. It is not just amusement or fun, but rather any activity apart from our regular work by which we re-create, that is, restore, energy of mind and body. We have gotten far from this meaning today. Recreation as most of us know it has become very commercialized, involving the expenditure of money for sports events, movies with their flagrant sex and violence, and night clubs and resorts. It has also become almost exclusively passive, with no active participation by those in attendance, and escapist in character, that is, removed from real-life situations. Anyone who watches television often or goes to the movies frequently will know what we mean.

Many types of modern recreation are not evil in themselves. Television and the movies are not wrong until they begin to promote and glorify the evils we have been talking about in this book. But as a channel of recreation, they leave much to be desired.

Recreation must become more creative. It must take on a more active character. It should become less commercialized. We must make an effort to bring a large part of family recreation back to the home. Family picnics and barbecues, a singalong, hobbies and crafts, dancing, games, making popcorn, coloring Easter eggs, making Christmas cards and tree ornaments, planting a garden, and countless other activities devised by imaginative parents and children can help greatly to strengthen the family bond. Do not neglect educational and cultural activities either. Reading, classes in religious and secular subjects, discussions of current events can provide an intellectual challenge to members of the family.

Families might set aside at least one day, or night, each week to engage in some planned activity. It could be one of those mentioned above or could involve away-from-home activities, including swimming, skating, fishing, bicycling, hiking, camping, viewing historical sights, and visiting museums, zoos, farms, dairies, and amusement parks. Some of these outings are free, a significant factor for budget-conscious families. But whatever the activity, the spirit in which it is carried out is more important than the activity itself.

A word of caution: Organized activities for children are numerous today and begin at an early age. They not only take children away from the family and parental influence but often demand so much time of one or two members of the family that the rest of the household suffers as far as recreational and social activities are concerned. These organized outside activities are wholesome and healthy for children, but parents must be careful to balance the interests of individual members of the family with the unity and togetherness of the whole family.

Family recreation should be fun. It does not have to involve only special events; it can mean just a happy family atmosphere, with laughter at meals, romps at bedtime, and wrestling on the floor. Carried out properly, family play can ease tensions, relieve boredom, soften discipline, and promote affection and understanding.

Lastly, this most important advice: *Enjoy the family God gave you while you have them with you.*

The four great bonds of marriage and parenthood — affection, common work, common prayer, and common play — can be the foundation for a successful and happy family life. When the modern family learns once more to work together, pray together, and play together affectionately, under the guidance of Christ, the unseen head of the household, our families will be well on their way toward becoming again a vital force for God and country.

A FEW FAMILY PRAYERS

PRAYER OF A MARRIED COUPLE

Almighty God, who has established and elevated the holy state of matrimony so that we, your creatures, might cooperate with you in fashioning citizens for heaven, and for our mutual help, consolation, and love, give us grace both thankfully to accept its blessings and faithfully to fulfill its duties. May your assistance continue in our union through our married life; help us to live together in love and peace, and aid us to fulfill faithfully our duties to you, to each other, and to our home.

Lord Jesus Christ, you gave a special dignity to family life by spending thirty years of your own life within a family; may the Holy Family of Nazareth be our model.

Accompany us, Lord, in all the daily actions of this life to which you have called us, and grant that the tie by which you have bound us together may ever grow stronger. Help us to be generous in giving ourselves for each other and making our home the best loved place of all. May you be our constant guide in the sacrifices we are called upon to make, and in the family trusts we must carry out.

And as you blessed the bridal couple at Cana by your presence, now bless our union and remain with us always; may we never forget you, the giver of all blessings. May our married life and home on earth lead us to our eternal home with you in heaven. Amen.

PRAYER FOR GUIDANCE
IN CHOOSING A STATE OF LIFE

Almighty God, you know that in my heart I have a sincere desire of pleasing you and of doing your will in all things. Help me now through the intercession of Mary, my mother, to know what state of life I ought to choose. When I have determined it, grant me the grace and strength to follow it through, so that my life may be in accord with your divine plan, that I may work out my own salvation and bring others closer to you. Through Jesus Christ Our Lord. Amen.

PRAYER FOR PURITY

Lord Jesus Christ, you who love to look upon a chaste soul and a pure character, you who took upon yourself our human nature through the Immaculate Virgin Mary, look down mercifully upon my infirmity. Grant me a clean heart, O God, and renew a wholesome spirit to conquer every sinful desire. Grant me a filial fear and a devoted love of you and your immaculate Mother, so that this enemy may be overcome, and that I may serve you with a chaste body and please you with a pure heart. Amen.

Immaculate Heart of Mary, pray for us.

PRAYER OF A MODERN PARENT

Lord Jesus Christ, you have seen fit to bless our marriage with children, and to entrust them to our care to raise them for you and prepare them for heaven. Give me your grace and help to be successful in carrying out this sacred trust. Teach me the right things to do; show me when to correct and when to praise or encourage; help me to be understanding, yet firm; considerate, yet watchful; guide my actions from either being too indulgent or too severe. Help me to show my children by word and example, the ways of wisdom, purity, holiness, and wholesomeness.

O Mary, stay close to our family and obtain for our children your Son's blessings, so that under our guidance they may grow in grace and love. Help us in guiding our children to keep the commandments more perfectly. Help us to worthily fill our role as God's partners in preparing souls for heaven, in so bringing up our children that they may be our joy in this world and our glory in the next. Amen.

THE PRAYER OF A YOUNG BRIDE
ON HER WEDDING DAY

This prayer was found among the personal effects of a young bride who died during an operation for appendicitis. She was only twenty-five years old, and had been married fourteen months.

O Father, my heart is filled with a happiness so wonderful I am almost afraid. This is my wedding day. I pray you that the beautiful joy of this morning may never grow dim with the tears of regret for the step I am about to take. Rather may its memories become more sweet and tender with each passing anniversary.

You have sent me the one who seems all worthy of my deepest regard. Grant me the power to keep him ever true and loving as now. May I prove indeed a helpmate, a sweetheart, a friend, a steadfast guiding star among all the temptations that beset the impulsive heart of mine.

Give me skill to make home the best loved place of all. Help me to make its light gleam rather than any glow that would dim its radiance. Let me, I pray you, meet the little misunderstandings and cares of life more bravely.

Be with me as I start my mission of womanhood, and stay my path from failure all the way. Walk with us even to the end of our journey. O, Father, bless my wedding day, hallow my marriage night, sanctify my motherhood if you see fit to grant me that privilege. And when all my youthful charms are gone and cares and lessons have left their traces, let physical fascination give way to the greatest charm of companionship.

And so may we walk hand in hand down the highway of the valley of the shadow which we will be able to lighten with the sunshine of good and happy lives. Father, this is my prayer. Hear me, I beseech you. Amen.

*A mirror of the expectations
of the men and women
of our time.*
— Pope Paul VI, March 22, 1974.

CHAPTER 9

The Modern Woman

In contemplating Mary and her mission . . . different generations of Christians, looking on her as the new woman and perfect
Christian, found in her as a virgin, wife, and mother the outstanding type of womanhood and the preeminent exemplar of life
lived in accordance with the Gospels and summing up the most
characteristic situations in the life of a woman. — Pope Paul VI,
Cult of Mary, February 2, 1974, No. 36

If we turn back the pages of man's history to the days before Christ and
Mary walked this earth of ours, we see that the position of woman was
indeed not an enviable one. The universal attitude was that a woman was a
creature inferior to man, her purpose on earth being little more than a
servant. She was completely excluded from public life, expected only to
hold a spot within the four walls of her own household and even there she
was to hold an inferior place, indeed a degraded place. She received little or
no education. Among pagans she was considered a chattel that could be
bought and sold. She could not choose her own marriage partner. And in
marriage she was not a companion but a servant whose life was little better
than that of a slave. A woman wronged or mistreated by her husband had
nowhere to turn for redress. And even in the so-called cultured nations
such as Greece or Rome, women were for the most part looked upon as inferior. The world-renowned philosopher Aristotle referred to a woman as
a subordinate creature. And Demosthenes frankly and brutally remarked:
"We have woman friends for entertainment, but wives for children and
household." Wives were given the place of servants in the household; prostitutes held a prominent place in the social life of Greece and Rome. Such a
philosophy of life dragged womanhood down to the depths of degradation.

This ancient pagan attitude toward women perseveres in some cases to modern times. A missionary from British East Africa related that in Uganda a man's wealth is measured by the number of wives he has. He will support as many women as he can afford. If one of them dies, she is put upon a litter, carried to the jungle, and thrown to the hyenas. If on the other hand the man dies, his grave is carefully dug at his hut. He is buried under a certain amount of earth, and the remainder of the grave is filled with great stones, in order to protect his body from the hyenas! Indeed a strange custom, vividly picturing for us the position of women in a pagan land.

AMONG THE JEWS

And even among the Jews of old, God's chosen people, whose moral outlook was on a much higher level, there was the idea that women should hold an inferior place.

Women were considered less capable of spiritual development than men — an idea that we, of later times, can see is utterly ridiculous. As a result of this belief, they were not permitted to worship in the synagogues with men. They were put aside in a separate room reserved for them. It was considered an act of impiety to impart the words of the Law to a woman.

A Jewish man would not greet a woman on the streets. He would not even talk to his own wife or daughter on the street. There was a certain kind of fanatical Pharisee who went about with his eyes closed, lest he should see a woman.

It was the woman alone who went to the well for water. A man considered himself disgraced if he should be seen carrying home water.

In morning prayer, a Jewish man would thank God, who had not made him "a gentile, a slave, or a woman."

Into such a world, Mary was born. In a humble house at Nazareth one day there resounded the words: "Rejoice, O highly favored daughter! The Lord is with you. Blessed are you among women." This greeting of heaven to a simple teenage girl brought with it a revolutionary change and a singular lasting honor for womanhood. Christ chose a woman to be an indispensable instrument in the redemption of the world. Divine recognition was given to womanhood and a world-wide change was to take place. Today every "Hail Mary" that is uttered is not only an expression of praise of her who is "Blessed among women," but a reflected expression of honor, of divine recognition and esteem for every woman.

CHRIST'S TRIBUTE

From Bethlehem to Calvary for thirty-three years, our Lord paid Mary his personal tribute of reverence, love, and honor. This example of Christ united to the life of Mary, the model and exemplar for womanhood, gave a new meaning, a new place of importance to every woman. And since that time the Catholic Church has held before the world those ideals.

Christianity put woman in her rightful place in the world. We are apt to take the place of women in the Gospel for granted. In light of the history of the world before the time of Christ, it can be seen that he revolutionized the position of women.

Picture to yourself a little town among the green hills in the southern part of Palestine. Off to one side of the town, a crooked path winds part way up the hill to a small, plain house surrounded by the bright scarlet flowers so common in the Holy Land.

On the path a figure is seen making its way up the hill. It is a young Jewish girl, not yet twenty years of age. She walks quietly and thoughtfully, for she bears within her body the Body of a Child conceived only a few short weeks before by the miraculous power of God. The girl is Mary, the Mother of God, and the Child is Christ, the Son of the Eternal Father.

Mary enters the house, which is that of her cousin Elizabeth. The two women exchange a holy greeting, Elizabeth rejoicing with Mary because of the great favor that God has granted her, and Mary humbly speaking the praises of God. Mary remains with her cousin for three months, and then finally returns to her home at Nazareth.

The story of the Visitation is as simple as that. It seems almost of no consequence. Certainly the Gospel story of the life of Christ would be complete without it. But Saint Luke seems to include it because the days of Mary's pregnancy were such holy days.

And so, year after year, the Church celebrates the feast of the Visitation of Mary to her cousin Elizabeth. It is not a feast that calls to our mind some great essential link in the chain of God's plan for the redemption of mankind. No, it is simply a day on which we are reminded of the tremendous honor that God showed to Mary and through her to womankind.

A GOVERNOR'S TRIBUTE

Alfred E. Smith, governor of New York, on one occasion spoke these words of tribute publicly:

Our Blessed Mother had to the last degree all the qualities every man loves to find in a woman — a deep love for his interests, but no interference in his business. That is something he wants to attend to himself, but at the same time he wants someone to stand behind him for sympathy and encouragement. He makes a distinction between interference and cooperation. He does not want a woman's fingers in his business, but he does want her heart in it. This rare combination is found in Our Blessed Mother and that is one reason why she so much appeals to men.

She is recorded as having spoken only seven times in the Scripture. The last time was on the day our Lord began his public life. Her last words were: "Do whatever he tells you." From that moment on, as far as Scripture tells us, she said nothing.*

But for the rest of Christ's life, Mary was there, silently exercising her motherly influence and love.

Remember the incident of Christ, one day sitting by Jacob's Well in Samaria? The Apostles had gone into town to buy food. Our Lord was tired and resting alone when a woman approached to draw water. She went about her task just as if no one were there — after all she was a woman and he a man — in that land, at that time, there could be no question of opening a conversation or any friendliness exchanged between them. Then almost as a clap of thunder out of the blue, Christ broke the silence: "Give me a drink." The answer of the woman reflects the revolutionary stand Christ was introducing to the world: "How can you ask me, a Samaritan and a woman, for a drink?" Our Lord then went on to manifest his divinity to this Samaritan woman. Christ was throwing traditional standards aside — he was introducing to the world a new view toward womanhood. The teachings of Christ combined with the influence of Mary, gave to the world an entirely new concept of the position of women.

THE UNICORN AND THE VIRGIN

There is a fable almost two thousand years old, about a certain unicorn that no hunters could ensnare. A unicorn is an imaginary animal, something like a horse, but with one horn in the center of its head. The unicorn of the fable was too strong and too swift for the best hunters. One day, a young girl happened to be near when the hunters were trying to trap

*From an address delivered by Alfred E. Smith, at the Xavier Sodality in New York, December 11, 1938.

the animal, and strangely enough, the unicorn became tame and docile. The secret was this: "The girl was a virgin, and the animal always became tame in the presence of a virgin."

Early Christians liked to express their thoughts in fables. This fable they interpreted by explaining that Christ was the unicorn, and that no human power could bring him down from heaven until Mary's perfect purity induced him to come and dwell with us. The fable shows clearly their high regard for womanhood.

Today one of the great boasts of Communism is that it has emancipated women. A glance at history will show that it was not Communism in modern times but Catholicism two thousand years ago which gave to woman her rightful privileges, honors, and dignity.

Marx wrote: "Differences of age and sex have no longer any distinctive social validity. All are instruments of labor." The significant word here is "instrument." Human beings are reduced to the dignity of a plumber's wrench. Women were forced into being "emancipated" by working in mines and handling pneumatic drills.

WORDS OF A PAGAN

One of the great tributes to Catholic womanhood, was given by the pagan teacher of Saint John Chrysostom. That pagan was so impressed with the influence on Saint John by his mother that he exclaimed: "What wonderful women the Christians possess!"

Cardinal Mindszenty, just a short time before he was taken prisoner by the Communists, and subjected to torture for his faith over a period of years, had written a book entitled *The Face of the Heavenly Mother.* The book in forceful language speaks out in praise of Mary and womanhood and the tremendous power of both in the modern world. In one chapter, the Cardinal relates the story of the mother of the Old Testament and her seven sons who were slain for refusing to deny a principle of their religion. The Cardinal's comment on the story is: "How well this mother had reared her sons." The comment came to be a foreshadowing of Cardinal Mindszenty's own life, when through his own heroic imprisonment his mother continued to pray for him; when through his own torture for his faith his mother's influence shone forth.

For sixteen centuries woman enjoyed her rightful place in Christ's plan, with the world looking up to her in the spirit typified by the ideals of Sir Galahad fame. Woman was a model of devotion and love; a model of virtue and the spirit of sacrifice. The husband was the head of the family but she was the heart. She was the molder of the character of the young. Women were the inspiration for so many great men and so many saints.

AND THEN SOMETHING HAPPENED

And then something happened in the world to tear down these ideals of womanhood.

Four major factors in modern history combined to lower the ideals of Christian womanhood which had remained for some sixteen centuries since the time of Christ: the Industrial Revolution, the Feminist Movement, Secularism, Communism.

The Industrial Revolution took woman from her place in the home, took those qualities by which she served her family and earned the respect and honor of society, those qualities by which she was a model of devotion, love and sacrifice, and put them to work in the factory. Economic necessity forced women into labor and led them that much further from their womanly ideals.

Man and woman have an equal but distinct dignity and position. They have different vocations. They are partners in a common task with different jobs to do. The woman, just as the man, has the obligation to live a useful life. Indeed she is by no means destined to a life of idleness. Ordinarily her function is one of wife and mother, and this is usually an engrossing task. Nor is it true that women of higher social standing should have servants to do all their work while they remain idle. Ordinarily the man will devote his energies to his profession or occupation, the woman to being the soul of the home. The unmarried woman in the world has a right to live an independent life, but a life suited to her nature as a woman. By nature a woman is not meant to do whatever a man does, and when she attempts this she loses so much of feminine dignity.

The right order of family life demands that society be so set up that the man will earn what is needed to support a family, and that the woman will devote her energies to her womanly tasks.

The so-called Feminist Movement led women to seek equality — an equality based on a masculine pattern. Women began to usurp the functions of men, to do the jobs of men. G. K. Chesterton sums up the situation in the witty remark: "Twenty million women rose to their feet with the cry 'We will not be dictated to' and proceeded to become stenographers!" Woman rebelled against the confinement of the home, rebelled against her womanly qualities, and now finds herself confined to the assembly line of a factory, to an office job, to a career — to the detriment of her family.

Feminism is a movement working for the so-called "emancipation of women." We must again state that women have an unsurpassed dignity and inviolable rights. Her first right and duty is to be herself, to be a woman through and through and not to cast her nature aside by slavishly imitating man. Woman has a unique mission and role in life.

Feminism has insistently proclaimed that woman's inferiority is due to her connection with the home, and the result is a sort of inferiority complex by which many a modern woman looks to man's life as the ideal to which she should strive.

In the Christian concept, women are not men's rivals. Each has his own place, his own role to fill, and neither the country nor the family will be served when (as has happened in so many civilizations) the men become more effeminate or the women more masculine.

MODERN PAGANISM

The spirit of Secularism, by which God and the Church are excluded from family life, from school, from work, from daily life, has taken away the solid foundation from womanly virtue.

One modern writer has vividly depicted the influence of secularism on womanhood by referring to a beauty contest as a "human stock show." There is a striking comparison between the method of selecting a prize-winning Holstein and a young subject with sparkling eyes, perfect legs, and a model figure. One is put in mind of the slave markets of old when slave women were put before the public for inspection and then sold to the highest bidder. All of this is consonant with the pagan concept of old when women were considered as playthings, as chattel, not having souls. Catholicism placed the Mother of Christ before the world as an ideal to be imitated and loved. The qualities of the soul became more important than the qualities of the body. The pure woman became the first choice of good men in choosing a wife. Motherhood became noble and sacred. Men honored their women . . . gave up their seats for them. The average good man saw more in woman than face and form. He was attracted by goodness, purity, real womanliness as idealized in the one model for all womanhood, Mary, the Mother of Jesus. Do women today realize that movie producers, magazine and book publishers, television promoters are all too often working to drag down modern women from the pedestal on which they belong — working to gradually bring them down to animal level?

Pius XII, anticipating the coming degeneration in the status of womanhood, many years ago warned: Many a modern girl "will not listen to nor accept advice; at the slightest suspicion of 'protection' she rebels. . . . She has no notion that she needs it to safeguard her feminine dignity and her noble spirit. . . . She has of religion and piety only the merest veneer of pretended devotion, without substance, without depth."*

Madam Kollontai, at one time the Soviet Delegate to the original League of Nations, made this statement concerning love and womanhood: "Love is a glass of water one swallows to satisfy a thirst." What such a philosophy of life does to womanhood!

In one year in the city of Moscow, there were 57,000 births and 154,000 abortions! The United States is fast becoming a rival in this murderous practice. This works havoc with any ideals of motherhood.

And what is the result? We see the low ideals of womanhood manifested in so many ways which we have almost come to take for granted.

Symbolic of what has happened is an incident which occurred on a crowded bus. A young man got up to give his seat to a woman a few yards away. There was another man a few steps closer to the seat and he managed to get there first. The woman had lost the race!

There is a story of a man on a New York subway who got up and gave a woman his seat and she fainted. When she revived, she thanked him and he fainted. Such a humorous incident reflects what is happening to standards in our day.

THE MODERN OUTLOOK

Today the world seems to be reversed on its stand toward womanhood. A woman is praised for sharing in the production of an airplane or a deadly bomb, and all too often jeered at for sharing in the divine prerogative of producing a human life. It is as if we were to praise a renowned sculptor for producing dog houses instead of statues.

The affable Pope John XXIII urged the modern woman, while holding to her ideals of true womanhood, to use her womanly talents for the good of society:

Modern social structures are still far from allowing woman, in the exercise of her professions, to achieve the fulfillment of her personality, and they do not allow her to make the contribution which the Church and society expect from her. Hence the urgency of findig new solutions, if we are to achieve an order and a

*Address to International Association for the Protection of the Young Girl, 1948.

balance more commensurate with woman's human and Christian dignity. Hence, too, the need for Catholic women to become aware of their obligations. Such obligations do not end, as they did once upon a time, within the confines of the family circle. Woman's gradual ascent to all the responsibilities of a shared life requires her active intervention on the social and political plane. Woman is as necessary as man to the progress of society, especially in all those fields which require tact, delicacy, and maternal intuition.*

MAKING IDEALS A REALITY

Just as the influence of the simple Jewish girl of Nazareth completely changed the condition of the world two thousand years ago and left her stamp on the world for all time, so today Catholic women hold a place of prime importance in making the ideals of Christ and Mary a living reality. That can be done in proportion to the twentieth century woman's devotion to and imitation of Mary.

First, in her own personal life the modern woman must know and practice the divine ideals of womanhood as exemplified by Mary. If women would in their own daily lives live the ideals that Mary gave the world in her life, then the world would begin to acknowledge and reverence once again the sublime dignity of womanhood.

Second, women must rebuild the Christian family, giving it its proper dignity with its full spiritual vitality as the basic unit of society. It is largely the woman — the wife and mother — who sets the pace for developing real Christian life in the family. The writer Frederick Shannon paints a vivid picture of the role that women play in the forming of Christian family ideals and of molding life and characters: "No blocks of marble do they round into statues; no canvasses do they adorn with glowing colors; no books do they write with scholarly taste; no music do they compose with sweet strains; no platforms do they occupy with persuasive speech. Yet they are all these, and more, because they are God's disciples of the unexplored and the unexpressed. Sculptors, they chisel the veined marble of flesh and blood into living, breathing human statues; artists, they paint the colors of righteousness on undying souls; authors, they write the literature of godliness on the hearts of their sons; musicians, they sing the white song

---

*Address to participants in a course of studies on Woman and Society, *Osservatore Romano,* September 7, 1961.

of chastity into the souls of their daughters; orators, their lives speak so eloquently of the invisible things of God, that after quitting the world, they being dead, speak on from the high places of eternity."

Thirdly, the twentieth century woman, whether in religious life, living the single life in the world, or in the married state, can have an influence she may never suspect, by becoming a powerful example of the spirit of dedication, devotion to duty, and self-sacrifice.

The fewer sacrifices a woman is required to make, the less inclined she is to make even these few. But when a woman lives a life which is an example of self-sacrifice and generosity, she not only stimulates herself to further heights of virtue, but is an inspiration to all around her. Particularly is she an inspiration to her own family. Where will the heroes of our nation come from, unless we have heroines in our homes? When the women of a nation become soft, then we have good cause for concern. History tells us that sixteen out of nineteen nations that have fallen, decayed from within. Abraham Lincoln, with clear insight, remarked on one occasion that he was not afraid of America being conquered from without, but he was afraid of it being decayed from within.

One of woman's essential functions in the divine plan is to be a living example of self-sacrifice, of wholehearted devotion — to her family, to duty, to all the womanly ideals. Women will be successful in their task in proportion to their devotion to Mary, and to their imitation of her.

A prominent American woman, the editor of a national magazine for girls, was interviewed informally on the radio. The interviewer remarked, "I understand that besides being editor you also have two teenage girls." The answer came back almost angrily, like the crack of a rifle: "I don't like the way you put that. I am first and foremost a mother; I also happen to be an editor." That is putting first things first.

MARY'S PART

Mary is today very much misunderstood. So many think of Mary as merely a sweet person. Mary was more than that. She was strong, courageous, self-sacrificing. She lived her life in the shadow of the cross — after all, she knew the prophecies concerning the death of her Son better than any other living person. She knew the suffering ahead, yet never once faltered, but unhesitatingly went about her daily tasks, completely devoted to her womanly mission. To imitate Mary is not by any means to be merely a sweet person. To be like her means developing a strong character, to be a tower of strength influencing all those around you.

This fact was emphasized by New York Governor Alfred E. Smith in another of his glorious tributes to our Lady:

She brought him into the world under the most terrible conditions of childbirth — in a stable — because there was no room for her in the inn. She carried him over burning sands and under scorching skies into Egypt. She sought him sorrowing when he was lost and found him in the temple about his Father's business. She knew what happened in the Garden of Gethsemane. She knew of the tragedy that was enacted on the porch of the palace of Pilate when he was scourged, spat upon and crowned with thorns. Remember — he was once her little boy. She loved him as only the perfect mother can love. What must have been the anguish that tore her heart when she met him on the road to Calvary just after he had fallen for the first time under the weight of the Cross she was afterwards to see him nailed upon. She saw the soldier drive the spear into his Sacred Heart and she saw the last drop of his precious blood fall upon the soil of Calvary to the end that we may all have eternal life.

Men love her because she braved the battle all the way from the Crib of Bethlehem to the Cross on Calvary. No person aside from her divine Son ever suffered more than she, and that is why we call her the Queen of Martyrs. Men love her because she was brave. She did not collapse, for John, who was there, tells us that she stood. Where were Peter, James, Andrew and the other Apostles? The truth is man was weak, woman was strong, and because she was strong she rallied men to the banner of her divine Son, and on Pentecost Sunday we find her in the midst of the Apostles, abiding in prayer. It was around woman that the manhood of the Church gathered then, and it is so even to this hour.*

RUSSIA AND MARY

We who sometimes take Mary's place for granted, might learn a lesson from a people who are now having every obstacle put in their path to prevent them from living these ideals. In the Catholic household of Russia there are many religious pictures, and whenever possible a picture of Mary hangs in the eastern corner of the bedroom and before it a vigil light burns. Here the life of the family begins and ends; here the groom brings his bride

*From an address delivered by Alfred E. Smith, to the Xavier Sodality in New York, December 11, 1938.

to kneel before the face of Mary and ask her blessing on their marital love; here they kneel to pray, thanking God for each child with which he blesses their marriage; here the children kneel and learn their little prayers; here will be uttered the last words before death of father, mother or child. Mary holds a place as the center of the household.

In Russia, there is a traditional custom of remembering Mary in one's will. Rich and poor have willed their most precious possessions to her. That is why so many churches in Russia have been so richly decorated with gold and silver and jewels.

There is an old Russian greeting: "May the peace of God be with you," and an old farewell runs, "May the blue mantle of Our Lady cover you with its gracious folds and keep you safe."

Several years ago newspapers carried accounts of a Catholic girl who heroically resisted the advances of a young man. A picture of the Blessed Virgin hung on the wall of the room where she was expected to surrender to his demands. "How can I commit this sin?" the girl insisted. "The picture of my Mother looks reprovingly on me." Not long after in despair the young man, once a Catholic, seized a revolver, turned the face of Mary's picture to the wall, and shot himself. He could not bear, he wrote in a note before he died, Mary's face looking on him disapprovingly.

Are today's women going to turn Mary's picture away from them when her image casts a reproving glance in the direction of modern womanhood? Or are our women going to keep Mary's likeness before them, presenting her as a model and their own life as an example to the rest of the world?

A modern philosopher a few years ago made this statement: "There is nothing in an age that so sharply mirrors its philosophy as the lives of its women." By that standard, how does our age measure up? Do the lives of its women mirror a way of life of which we can be proud?

DIFFERENCE BETWEEN MEN AND WOMEN

While urging women to take their proper place in society, Pope John XXIII proclaimed the primacy of values, emphasizing that women have a different function from men. This Pope reflects the thoughts of many Supreme Pontiffs before him and the reminder of the Church in our day:

Any consideration of a woman's occupation cannot disregard the unmistakable characteristics with which God has marked her nature. It is true that living conditions tend to bring almost complete equality of the sexes. Nevertheless, while their justly-proclaimed equality of rights must extend to all the claims of personal and human dignity, it does not in any way imply equality of functions. The Creator endowed woman with natural attributes, tendencies, and instincts, which are strictly hers, or which she possesses to a different degree from man; this means that woman was also assigned specific tasks.

To overlook this difference in the respective functions of men and women or the fact that they necessarily complement each other, would be tantamount to opposing nature: the result would be to debase woman and to remove the true foundations of her dignity.

We should also like to remind you that the end for which the Creator fashioned woman's entire being is motherhood. This vocation to motherhood is so proper to her and so much a part of her nature that it is operative even when actual generation of offspring does not occur. Therefore, if women are to be assisted in their choice of an occupation, and in preparing and perfecting their qualifications, it is necessary that, in the practice of their profession, there be some means for continuously developing a maternal spirit.

What a contribution to society it would be if she were given the opportunity to use these precious energies of hers to better advantage, especially in the fields of education, social work, and religious and apostolic activity, thereby transforming her occupations into various forms of spiritual motherhood! Today's world has need of maternal sensibilities to dispel the atmosphere of violence and grossness in which men are often struggling.*

The world is filled with crime and sin. In the press, the theater, in books, on the radio and television, the noble ideals of womanhood are being attacked. In such a world which is flaunting morality, today's women must defend the standards of Christ and Mary. Today's women must reject sinful fashions aimed at arousing the lower passions of men; they must live so as to inspire men to look on womanhood with pure eyes; today's women must rebuild the ideals of marriage. By and large, women will set the moral standards of society. Today's women, if they are to fulfill their mission, must dare to be different.

There is more truth than we might suspect in the old proverb: "The hand that rocks the cradle is the hand that rules the world." In the Catho-

---

*Address to participants in a course of studies on Woman and Society, *Osservatore Romano*, September 7, 1961.

lic pattern, women hold a lofty and important spot, and a place with far-reaching responsibilities. A woman need not be in the public eye, in politics, or in business to influence the world. "Not in the branches of a tree but in its roots do force and power reside." Woman is a powerful influence in the roots of society. When those roots become strong, pure, and healthy, then society will manifest a new life.

The formula is simple. Mary, a humble girl, living in an obscure town, left a lasting imprint on womanhood, on family life, and on the world. Today the life of a Catholic woman will have a similar effect on the world insofar as her life is a reflection of Mary's. That ought to be the ideal of every woman.

The remark of G. K. Chesterton reflects a fundamental truth: "The important thing for a country is that men should be manly, the women womanly." And how better can true Christian womanliness become a reality than through the influence of Mary?

"Woman has the awful choice of being Eve or Mary; she is rarely neutral," said Cardinal Suenens. "Either she enobles and raises man up by her presence, by creating a climate of beauty and human nobility, or she drags him down with her in her own fall."*

The power of a woman! However we may express the truth, the basic idea has a tremendous significance in our own day.

*Suenens, Cardinal Leo: *The Nun in the World,* p. 15.

CHAPTER 10

The
Senior Citizen
in Today's Society

Age is opportunity no less
Than youth itself, though in another dress,
And as the evening twilight fades away
The sky is filled with stars, invisible by day.
— Henry Wadsworth Longfellow,
Morituri Salutamus, stanza 24

SECTION 1

In our day when the span of life is extending and the number of older people is increasing, we have more and more come to be a youth-oriented society. There are cultures that are very different. Think of the Chinese. It would be considered a disgrace and socially reprehensible for a Chinese family to refuse to assume the responsibility of aging relatives. Indeed, the younger generation looks to the elderly to benefit from their wisdom and experience. The Jewish and Italian family and social traditions are much the same in attitudes toward the elderly.

Among so many other societies today, the upcoming generation looks to put aside older people, and the older people consider that their productive years and time of fulfilling activities are over.

TWO VIEWPOINTS

Our viewpoints on the senior citizen in today's society are from two aspects: the attitude of the younger and middle aged toward the elderly; the attitude of the elderly toward their own life.

Like a drop of sea water,
like a grain of sand,
so are these few years among
the days of eternity.
— (Sir. 18:8).

At the outset, the keynote of social and religious attitudes and obligations might be given in several reminders from the Bible and the Vatican Council II:

Cast me not off in my old age; as my strength fails, forsake me not. — Psalm 71:9.

Stand up in the presence of the aged and show respect for the old. — Leviticus 19:32.

Among the multiple activities of the family apostolate may be enumerated the following . . . help for the aged not only by providing them with the necessities of life but also by obtaining for them a fair share of the benefits of economic progress. — Vatican II *Decree on the Apostolate of the Laity,* No. 11.

And now that I am old and gray, O God, forsake me not till I proclaim your strength to every generation that is to come. — Psalm 71:18.

With these thoughts as a background, we must not just make an appeal to the younger generation to give reverence and care for their elders. Rather, the older generation must deepen the incentive to enrich their lives and ours, and give what only they can give to the world and to the younger generation. The elderly have more experience, wisdom, and time for study, prayer, and apostolic work. Too few utilize these assets.

THE CHALLENGE OF GROWING OLD

As a foundation to our thoughts, let us say that growing older ought to be looked upon not as a sentence to which one is consigned, but rather as a challenge.

Older people usually have more time for study, thought, fulfilling reading and helpful activity. The time-consuming task of bringing up a family is over, the hours of commitment to a job to make a living may be finished. It is unfortunate that so many waste these years in just putting in time, in self-pity, in passive television viewing.

There is a massive supply of inexpensive books, the best of reading available. In addition to secular books, there are numerous religious works.

Nowadays classes are offered in arts and crafts. Retirement can be a time of acquiring new skills and satisfying hobbies. And many of these may be utilized not only for self-satisfaction but to help others. Production of ceramics, photographic works or electronic skills might be utilized to bring income for a senior citizens club with varied activities. Bookkeeping and clerical skills might be put to good use either on a voluntary basis or to bring a minimal income through one's own parish, school or diocesan apostolic agency. The local home for the aged might use an older person's skills in almost any field, including painting, tailoring, carpentry and electricity. A person who has developed some skill through his life, or who is willing to acquire a new skill, can be of great use in his own local area in a charitable or social service agency. There is no need to "rust away."

GROWTH IN HOLINESS

Retirement years, with more leisure time, can and should be used for growth in prayer and the spiritual life. Again, many books are available to deepen one's spiritual life and bring a person closer to God. Along this line, often older persons have physical afflictions and, not uncommonly, are troubled by loneliness. Both can be utilized in a spirit of sacrifice to grow spiritually. Priests, ministers, rabbis and lay persons actively engaged in apostolic work often forget that a major powerhouse of spiritual help can come just through a request to the elderly. Just ask them to back up your activity with their prayers and sacrifices; they will feel needed and you will feel the results.

With more available time, older people need not merely sit home and pray. There are unlimited apostolic activities in which they can set their own pace. Regular visits can be made to the sick, and to those living alone right in one's own parish or city. Many nursing homes welcome regular visits to their patients. Baby-sitting can free young couples for active apostolic work, or for needed relaxation. Census work and house visiting for your own parish help to ease the burden of the priests and sisters.

One fruitful apostolate for older people is writing. Some may have a talent for writing articles for publication, and almost all have the capability of letter writing. This can be engaged in even by one who is somewhat confined either to home or in a home for the aged. The apostolate of the pen is largely overlooked these days. Letters to legislators concerning desired laws; letters to television stations or sponsors commending good programs and protesting harmful or immoral ones; letters to city officials bringing to their attention needed reforms; or just letters to people who are sick or lonely. A person who has nothing to do, might take on the project of "a letter a day to someone." In the course of a year, an enormous amount of good can be accomplished.

GET INVOLVED

Perhaps the most common and critical problem facing those in later years is loneliness. A particular effort should be made by the person himself and by his friends and relatives to pursue contacts with friends and to take steps to develop new contacts and continuing relationships. Regular visits and telephone calls to fellow-seniors who are living alone will be fruitful on both sides. Becoming involved in service to others either through organizations or on a person-to-person basis will be rewarding. Senior citizens clubs are on the increase and should be utilized.

But with all this, a person may still feel somewhat isolated. It is then one may finally realize that it is only by turning to God that true solace can be found. Christ knew loneliness in the Garden of Gethsemani and felt abandonment on the cross. A great sense of consolation, hope, optimism and joy can be gained by the thought of the presence of God. For a Catholic, this reaches its highest degree of perfection by spending time in the presence of the Blessed Sacrament. This might be in some nearby church or chapel; or, if one is fortunate, in a Catholic Residence, where there is a private chapel. Hopefully a person would not wait to utilize this as a last resort, but cultivate a closer relationship with Christ through the years.

Not uncommonly a man or woman comes to a point in life which is by no means extreme old age and says, "My time for accomplishment is finished." A reminder of men who made their greatest achievements in later life can serve as an inspiration. Verdi, Hayden and Handel gave the world great music after the age of 70. Rembrandt painted some of his masterpieces toward the end of his life. Einstein and Schweitzer made their mark on the world late in life. Cardinal Farnese at 68 was bent double, walked with a cane, and appeared to be nearing the end of his life; but upon his election as Pope Paul III, he straightened up and reigned for 15 years. Pope Clement XII was 78 when he was elected, and he reigned until he was 88.

Another frequent plague of old age is worry. Many are concerned about past wrongdoings; they are worried about their present circumstances; there is much anxiety about what the future will bring, particularly a concern about security. Such should take heart from the reminder of Christ: "Do not worry about your livelihood, what you are to eat or drink or use for clothing. . . . Look at the birds in the sky. They do not sow or reap, they gather nothing into barns; yet your heavenly Father feeds them" (Mt. 6:25-26). Christ does not want anxious Christians or worrisome Christians. He looks for tranquil and joyous Christians. It is a deepening of a dependence upon Christ which can bring this to us. "Come to me, all you who are weary and find life burdensome, and I will refresh you" (Mt. 11:28). Remember, too, that the priest is Christ's representative; take your worries to him, especially in the sacrament of penance.

Two crises, often in combination, can beset the elderly: facing the unexpected, and a developing sense of resentment. It might be the need for a move to a new place of residence, the death of a relative, or the abandonment of a friend. Age makes it more difficult to adjust to the unexpected, and both the older person himself and the younger people around him should realize this. Sometimes it develops into resentment of God. "I have tried to do right but nothing seems to go right in my life." Or, "What have I done to deserve this?" A visit to hospitals or homes for the elderly will usually bring stories of how relatives, friends or God, have "failed" the patients. There is nothing that can give a balance better than faith in God. He knows best. A kind word or a willing ear can help.

THE NEED TO BE NEEDED

Freud's teaching that people are primarily driven on and influenced in their goals by sexual drive, is called into question by many, perhaps most, today. Some psychologists today insist that the primary incentive is the search for meaning in life. Many an older person has lost this sense of a meaning to his life. "I am of no use anymore." That person must see and those around him must help him to feel a sense of being needed, a sense of usefulness in his life. A modern nursing home with air conditioning and television and every modern comfort — but without a staff, relatives and friends who give a sense of meaning and usefulness to the lives of its patients, is not fulfilling its purpose. An aging grandmother or grandfather who is put aside in a beautiful room, but whose advice is never sought, or whose baby-sitting is never asked for, or whose help around the house is rejected, can easily come to feel that life is without meaning. What a waste that a person puts himself on a shelf — or that others put him on a shelf — to vegetate, when there is wisdom, love, experience and perhaps talent just for the asking.

Francois Mauriac was a world-renowned novelist who died at the age of 84. He wrote his own eulogy in which were the words: "I believe as I did when I was a child, that life has meaning, direction, value; that no suffering is lost, that every tear counts, and each drop of blood; that the secret of the world is to be found in St. John's words, 'God is love.' " May our country which values the vitality and idealism of youth, come to recognize the experience, stability, devotion and spiritual wellspring of age; may our youth in their zeal to accomplish good and the restoration of social justice, come to respect the wisdom that only age can give; may our senior citizens recognize what they have to offer society, and though they may have retired from a job, may they not retire from constructive living and activity. As the youthful Mary of the Gospels visited the aging Elizabeth to honor her on the occasion of her giving a new life to the world, so may our society come to pay honor to our aging men and women as they by their lives give new vitality to our world.

A PRESENT FROM VIRGINIA

Several years ago, a priest friend of ours, who made a special apostolate of visiting hospital patients, related an incident which in its own simple way reveals something that is in the depth of every human heart. Virginia was a little girl nine years of age. She had saved some money to buy her mother a Christmas present. As the big day drew near, Virginia left the house to go to a store and buy the present. Crossing a street, she was struck by a car. Fortunately, the injuries were not very serious. As Virginia's mother sat by the hospital bed, she said to the young girl, "I don't need a present, Virginia; all I need is you."

No matter how old your parents are, no matter how old you are, they need you and you need them. Presents, money, air conditioning, television sets, beautiful rooms, will not mean a thing without love for each other. "It is love that makes the world go 'round." And that is true whether you are nine or ninety.

SECTION 2

Following are some suggestions for meeting the needs of the elderly. These have been compiled and written for this book by the Little Sisters of the Poor, who since 1839 have cared for over 45,000 elderly throughout the world. There are today over 4,900 Little Sisters on five continents, conducting over 290 Homes for the Elderly. In the United States, there are over 45 Homes spread out from the Atlantic to the Pacific coast, and from Minnesota to New Orleans.

WHAT ARE THE ELDERLY REALLY LIKE?

Elderly people do think clearly, but a little more slowly. It will take time for them to grasp the full significance, but when they do, their judgments are accurate and their suggestions good.

Elderly people have keen recall for the past, but have difficulty learning new things. However, they can learn them, and sometimes enjoy doing so.

Elderly people — at least those with religious sentiments — usually have a realistic attitude toward life and also toward death. They are not afraid of death and are glad when they can help others by prayers and their presence to die well. Relatives and staff in institutions have more difficulty with it.

Elderly people have the same human needs as any other person. . . . They must have love, respect, recognition and a sense of usefulness, if their old age is to be positive, if it is to be good.

Elderly people understand their limitations, but they are also quick to see through artifice. They will read the heart of what is said with the lips, and this works for both good intentions which are perhaps expressed awkwardly, as well as for a pretended interest.

The chief sufferings of the elderly are not physical. Yes, there are rough days for them because of physical ailments, but the chief sufferings are a sense of rejection, uselessness, loneliness and grief. A small thought . . . a card . . . a visit . . . an expression of appreciation . . . do more than a mountain of aspirin for ailing spirits. The finest surroundings are meaningless to the elderly, just as they are to children and adults, if they are void of warmth, love and concern. Elderly people adjust to the most unusual conditions well and cheerfully, if love and understanding are there. They especially need a peaceful and serene, secure environment, which for many is found in religious expressions.

Old is a relative term and there are few elderly who really consider themselves "old," so long as life holds out to them purpose. And because the Christian elderly are Christian, there is no such thing as a useless human being. They can be the backbone of society and the support of the Church by the proper use of this time of their lives. In order to do this, however, many of them require the encouragement of religious leaders and persons who sincerely believe this to be true.

GENERALITIES

The elderly, understood as over 65, constitute a large segment of the population, in round figures about 10% of the total population. Women outnumber men by approximately 33%. Less than one-third of these are employed beyond the age of 65 years. A vast number of the employed elderly are those with higher education. Unemployment rises sharply for unskilled or semi-skilled workers after this age due to forced retirement.

FINANCES

The married elderly seem to be somewhat better off than the unmarried; and of the unmarried, men are usually better off than women. Income drops greatly with the onset of 65.

INSTITUTIONALIZATION

Of the total number of elderly, only about 5% are institutionalized. The average age of those seeking institutionalization has risen to 80 years or better. The factors which require this institutionalization can be very varied and the adjustment of the individual to this process will be directly related to the reasons for which it is accomplished.

SOME REASONS FOR INSTITUTIONALIZATION

1. Concern on the Part of the Family
   a) Old person lives alone; becoming feeble or unable to carry out life functions (shopping, cooking).
   b) Parent will not live with children; parent incompatible with children due to personality clashes or changes due to advancing years; parent unable to live with children due to unavailable living quarters, size of families, or working child and marriage partner.
   c) No living relatives to assume responsibility.
   d) Desire for companionship of own age (usually as a means to combat depression, loneliness).
2. Lack of Concern on the Part of the Family
   a) Child and parent have been alienated over a long period of time (perhaps due to alcoholism, or a second marriage which was unfortunate for the child).
   b) Great distance separates them (not always real lack of concern, but has same effect).
   c) Inability of the parent to accept the lifestyle of the child, giving rise to great unhappiness for both.
3. Self-Determination of the Elderly
   a) They want to come for companionship, security, religious motives.
4. The Mental or Physical State of the Individual Requires It
   a) This last factor was mentioned last, deliberately. Nursing Home

so due to the emotional drain and the inability to adapt. A sense of rejection by loved ones is crucial to the death or deterioration process.

GOD'S LITTLE ONES, HIS POOR ONES

The Little Sister of the Poor, due in large part to the charisma of her foundress, Jeanne Jugan, views the elderly as God's "Anawim". . . . his "little" ones. . . . his "poor" ones. . . . regardless of their age, personality or social status. Therefore, she believes that they are especially dear to him and loved by him and she wishes to communicate this message to them. She must be wise with the wisdom of the world, simple as the dove, but above all, she must learn to use human means but always rely on divine help.

The goal of the Little Sister is to use the human conditions existing in order to create a spiritual atmosphere of peace, serenity, purposefulness, love and understanding. She comes to read the heart of the elderly rather than the words they utter. . . . to find the depth below the surface. . . . to see the image of Godliness masked by the forces which environment, heredity, grief, emotional depravation, and insecurity have produced on the physiognomy. She comes to know that the person she sees has all the human needs of any other human being, following the dictum, "Men are more alike than not alike," and that, as the years advance, the "why" of life becomes more crucial. The solution also becomes more simple, in that the elderly turn more readily to things spiritual and grasp their significance with an astounding ease.

The Little Sister tries to create a milieu that says "Home." I am "Home." This Home is a foretaste of my eternal Home. This Home radiates the qualities of a Christian Home; it has love, stability, mutual respect and concern, an air of "otherliness."

There is joy in the simple events of life. . . . a birthday, a visit. There is meaningfulness to daily life. . . . "I can help" . . . through some familiar chore, assisting a companion, praying for the needs of others, participating in the crafts programs. The talents of early life have a usefulness. . . . "I can still repair the plug, mend the dress, make a baby sweater for my neighbor's grandchild, reassure my companions and just cheer them up with talking and listening to the "old days" relived.

The status of the elderly person as a decision-maker is respected. He is part of the running of the home. He has a say in the programs he wishes were carried out. Some need help to reassume active lives; others prefer less social life. Each has his place and each is respected as an individual.

However, no home for the elderly will ever supplant the affection of

institutionalization often takes this causality, but this is sometimes, if not frequently, only a contributing factor and not the
primary one.
  b) Senility is a most difficult condition. Adequate facilities are sel-
      dom available for the senile. Many are placed in psychiatric in-
      stitutions due to a lack of any better living arrangement.

ADJUSTING TO A NEW LIFESTYLE

1. The elderly person who is institutionalized goes through a "disen-
    gagement process" more or less severe depending upon several factors.
    a) The personality structure.
    b) The willingness with which the transfer is made. Experience
        shows that the resident who is admitted but for whom the ad-
        mission was misrepresented (i.e. a visit, a vacation, a short stay,
        etc.), usually, if not always, will adjust poorly, even to becoming
        agitated, disoriented or psychotic. The same thing happens
        frequently when the individual has been living alone in a very
        non-stimulating environment, with few personal contacts, and
        who has beginning senile cerebral changes. Institutionalization
        seems to create severe orientation problems and based on the
        basic strength of the personality may cause rapid disintegration
        and disorientation, and produce senile psychotic symptoms.
        This has physical as well as mental and emotional manifesta-
        tions.
2. Those do best in adjustment to this new lifestyle who:
    a) Have been a part of the process of decision-making.
    b) Understand the reasons for it.
    c) Are assured of family concern and devotedness.
    d) Want this living arrangement — for any number of reasons
        (i.e., see it as a positive good).
    e) Have visited the facility, met some of the residents, are able to
        feel free in the new environment to live at least some of the im-
        portant (to them) lifestyle patterns they are accustomed to.
3. In all honesty, it would seem that "disengagement" takes place in al-
    most 100% of those admitted and that this is the biggest factor in ad-
    justment as well as survival. A "cliche" has it that if an elderly person
    survives the first year, his chances are good for adjustment. Death rate
    during the first year is highest for all deaths in the facility. Some are
    near this point, physically, on admission, but a large number become

loved ones, nor remove the ache of being forgotten or overlooked. The holidays are perhaps the hardest days for elderly residents. When memories abound, the absence of concern becomes acutely felt by the elderly. Not all are able to visit or return to their families at these times; and they cannot but feel forgotten if the days pass, and relatives are "too busy" to "squeeze in" a visit to them. "Thank God for the Nuns" or "Thank God for the Staff," may be very complimentary to the nuns and the staff, but is a sad reminder that something else was expected. The Little Sister tries to teach or recall to the resident the Christian value of such suffering when offered, when accepted, when used for the good of men. However, there is nothing that makes it a good in itself.

Divine Providence is the mainstay of the Little Sister and all the more so since it is the mainstay of the elderly, especially today. Confidence in God's watchful care comes from a profound conviction of his love for the Anawim. . . . the "remnant" of God's People. And as the situation becomes bleaker for the elderly, the dependence of the Little Sister on the only power that can really resolve it, only becomes stronger. "If God wills it, it will be done." This is her heritage and her belief.

CHAPTER 11

The Tenth Man in Our Midst

The Church rejects, as foreign to the mind of Christ, any discrimination against men or harassment of them because of their race, color, or condition of life. — Vatican II, *Declaration on the Relationship of the Church to Non-Christian Religions,* No. 5

The population of the United States is approximately nine per cent black. Add to this figure members of other racial minority groups and we realize that better than one man of every ten in our country is a member of a racial minority group. He has human rights as inalienable as those of the other nine.

Yet in this great country which proclaims equality and justice for all, is there anyone who can say in all sincerity: "We have no race problem?"

This question, so often brushed aside with a shrug, has world-wide, indeed eternal, repercussions.

Hitler, in a last pre-war conference with a high American diplomat, defended his treatment of the Jews by pointing out the American treatment of Negroes. And today, Communists throughout the world are using the Negro problem, the Puerto Rican problem, the Mexican problem, in their effort to discredit America before the eyes of the world. Indeed, this racial problem of ours has world-wide repercussions.

As for the eternal repercussions, we have merely to recall the frequent, clear reminders of our recent popes, official proclamations of the Church and indeed the teachings of the Bible itself.

All are one in Christ Jesus.
— (Gal. 3:28).

Archdiocese of Newark International Liaison

Diplomats and politicians, sociologists and economists, educators and religious leaders are all studying this problem of "the tenth man in our midst." The day has passed when we can take a neutral stand on racial issues. We can no longer ignore "the tenth man."

PRIESTS IN PRISON

It was the Feast of Christ the King. An archbishop ascended his pulpit — an archbishop being threatened by his government with arrest and the torture chamber for his insistent presentation of Catholic principles. Slowly he began to speak:

We assert that every people and every race which has been formed on earth today has the right to life and to treatment worthy of man. All of them without distinction, be they members of the Gypsy race or of another, be they Negroes or Europeans, be they Jews or Aryans, all have an equal right to say, "Our Father, who art in heaven." If God has granted this right to all human beings, what worldly power can deny it? Therefore the Catholic Church has always condemned and will always condemn every injustice and compulsion perpetrated in the name of social, racial and national theories.

These words were spoken by the late Cardinal Stepinac, who was shortly thereafter imprisoned by the Communist powers in Yugoslavia.

The Cardinal's words seem to re-echo those of another zealous priest who was also cast into prison. Saint Paul preached these same teachings of the Church in the simple words: "No more Jew or Gentile, no more slave or freeman. . . . You are all one person in Jesus Christ." Yes, Saint Paul knew that there were slave and free. He knew that there were different races. But he was saying that it makes no difference to God.

For many years, Monsignor McMinamin of Denver sponsored "Brotherhood Week." He wished to remind the country that all men — regardless of race or color or nationality — should be regarded as brothers under the fatherhood of God; that consequently there should be no antagonism between groups, and that prejudice is wrong.

A JEWISH THOUGHT

There is an ancient Jewish midrash to this effect:

"As I was walking in the desert, I saw an object in the distance. It appeared to be a tree. As I came closer, I thought it was a camel. As I came still closer, I saw it was a man. When I walked up to him, I saw that it was my brother."

As Catholics we must not be anti-Semitic, anti-Negro, anti-anybody, since the Catholic Church has always taken a clear stand on the question of prejudice.

With reference to anti-Semitism, on March 25, 1928, the Vatican declared: "The Catholic Church habitually prays for the Jewish people. . . . Actuated by this love the Apostolic See has protected this people against unjust oppression."

Pope Pius XII gave this strong reminder to the world: "The only road to salvation is definitely to repudiate all inordinate pride of race and blood." It is left for individual Catholics to put this Church teaching into practice.

The good or evil done to another must be considered as good or evil done to Christ. Remember the story of Saint Paul's persecution of the Church before his conversion? One day while riding to Damascus, he was struck to the ground and heard the voice of Christ saying: "Saul, why do you persecute me?" It was not Christ whom Paul was persecuting, but his followers — and yet those words rang in his ears: "Why do you persecute me?" And then he remembered what Christ had said about the Last Judgment, for in calling the just, Jesus will say:

Come. You have my Father's blessing! . . . For I was hungry and you gave me food, I was thirsty and you gave me drink. I was a stranger and you welcomed me. . . . Then the just will ask him: "Lord, when did we see you hungry and feed you or see you thirsty and give you drink? When did we welcome you?" . . . The king will answer them: "I assure you, as often as you did it for one of my least brothers, you did it for me." Then he will say to those on his left: "Out of my sight, you condemned. . . . I was hungry and you gave me no food, I was thirsty and you gave me no drink. I was away from home and you gave me no welcome." . . . Then they in turn will ask: "Lord, when did we see you hungry or thirsty or away from home . . . and not attend you in your needs?" He will answer them: "I assure you, as often as you neglected to do it to one of these least ones, you neglected to do it for me" (Mt. 25:34-45).

Of course there are people of all races who do evil things. No matter what your racial group may be, you must admit that some of your own people have done evil things! Make this distinction: We must hate the sin, but love the sinner. And make this further distinction: We do not have to like people, but we do have to love them, with the same sort of love that Jesus Christ loves us. And we are all sinners, every single one of us.

What about that black fellow-Christian you did not want in the pew with you in Church? What about that Jewish businessman towards whom you were uncharitable? What about that family you resented simply because they were white? What about the little Mexican girl you did not want in the Catholic school with your children? What about them?

God sees men's souls made to his own image and likeness, souls destined for heaven. All else is unimportant; it is accidental and does not affect human dignity. The twentieth century world is a far cry from Christ's standards in this regard. Christ proclaimed the fundamental principles that each of us is a child of the same Father, that everyone is redeemed by the same Blood of Christ, that all are brothers with one Father.

The attitude of the Godless is exemplified by an incident that occurred in Germany when Hitler was first coming into power. Near the town of Maria Laach, there was a sign over the entrance to a synagogue which read: "Have we not all one Father and one God?" The Nazis demanded that it be removed, because they considered it an insult that they should be said to have the same Father as the Jews.

What about Christ's teachings on social justice today? Are they being lived by those who profess to be Christ's followers?

MAKE THE TIME RIPE

The attitude of a Catholic, and indeed any person of good will, might well be guided by the words of Pope Pius XII in the encyclical *Sertum Laetitiae*. "We feel a special paternal affection, which is certainly inspired of heaven, for the Negro people. . . . In the field of religion and education, we know that they need special care and comfort and are very deserving of it. We therefore invoke an abundance of heavenly blessing and we pray fruitful success for those whose generous zeal is devoted to their welfare."

Pope Paul VI, in a terse statement, gave a reminder to the modern world of the need to get back to fundamentals for a solution to our social problems: "The world is sick. Its illness consists less in the unproductive monopolization of resources by a small number of men than in the lack of brotherhood among individuals." (*Development of Peoples,* March 26, 1967, No. 66).

In working toward a solution of modern social problems on a Christian basis, as in practically every other movement in the Church, there can be two camps: the first is the number of the over-zealous and imprudent; the second is the group comprising the over-timid. On the one side there are those who want to dash ahead without fully knowing what faces them;

on the other are those who are quite satisfied with the status quo, not too anxious for improvement or change. The two types may be compared to the accelerator and the brake of an automobile — neither one should be forgotten. Both are necessary if we hope to drive safely and to steer a middle course. That does not mean a compromising of principles, but necessitates a building of methods on a solid foundation. It neither means that we are content with the application of Christ's principles of social justice in the world today, nor that we are satisfied with the interracial situation as it is. It does mean that if we are to gain a lasting improvement, we ought to think things over prudently and know what we are about. We might well sum up the current situation in the words of the Rev. John LaFarge, S.J., outstanding apostle and authority in the field of interracial relations:

The time is overripe. Much of the difficulty we are in today is due to our careless drifting when we could have been charting our course. Time does not always grow sweeter with mere waiting; it sometimes grows sourer with its own maturity. Abuses are committed today which were not thought of forty or fifty years ago. Instead of serving as a convenient alibi, this maxim (that the time must be ripe) is a challenge. It is our job to act immediately to work and "make the time ripe" by our program of Catholic interracial education.

CHAPTER 12

America on Its Knees

Leave your gift at the altar, go first to be reconciled with your brother, and then come and offer your gift. — Words of Jesus Christ as recorded by Matthew (5:24)

Those who profess to be followers of Christ must take a firm stand in applying his principles of social justice in the world today. In our lives, we can never forget that Christianity is not simply a matter of avoiding sin. There is an old proverb that reminds us: "One does evil enough by not doing any good." There are many things that we must do. When a person on the last day finds himself standing before Christ, his Judge, and saying: "I did not murder, steal or commit adultery," Christ will ask: "But what did you do?" It is one thing to avoid injustice and uncharitableness in our own lives. It is quite another thing to do something about the violations of justice and charity taking place all around us.

Buried away in the pages of a magazine devoted to Chinese religion and culture, appeared this proverb: "The man who talks for both sides is not to be trusted by either." When we apply that axiom to the present-day Christian-racist, we can draw some interesting conclusions. The man who goes along with the tide of racial or national injustice and discrimination in his daily contacts, while trying to be a devout Catholic in church, professing to be a follower of the teachings of Christ, is attempting something which is contradictory. He has, so to speak, a religious split personality.

*Rich and poor
have a common bond:
the Lord is the maker of them all.
— (Prv. 22:2).*

photo by Richard B. Hoffman

Christianity, when lived to the full, and in particular Christ's doctrine of God and neighbor, will, when really put into practice, end this "spiritual schizophrenia." It will effectively resolve the present-day conflict between the spiritual and the social.

Not uncommonly a person comes to realize the shocking contradiction between racism and the fundamental principles of Christ, and exclaims: "Why doesn't the Catholic Church do something about it?"

Actually the Church is doing something about it. She speaks out daily in terms which are unmistakably clear in meaning. Yes, we use that word "daily" in its literal sense, for each day in the language of the liturgy, the Catholic Church eloquently proclaims lessons of interracial justice for Catholics to live. How can a Catholic who really understands the Holy Sacrifice of the Mass and the doctrine of Christ's Mystical Body, and who applies that knowledge in his own life, ever consciously violate social justice?

SIDE BY SIDE AT MASS

Helen Caldwell Day was a Negro nurse who became a Catholic in her twenties. She had experienced the fears, anxieties and sufferings of discriminatory practices. In these words, she told what the Catholic Faith and the Mass meant in her life:

> When I went to chapel to Mass in the morning, I lost all my self-consciousness, because I was no longer a stranger to these people but one with them. It was a wonderful thing to offer again with Christ and all the Christians of the world, his perfect sacrifice to his Father. When the priest raised our Lord, that we might adore him in the Host, I would think that even while we gazed upon him, we were part of his mystical body, members of him and of each other.*

Yes, the Mass and the mystical body of Christ can have far-reaching implications.

As I kneel before the altar, side by side with my fellow-Catholics ready to assist at Mass, I must remember that what I am about to do is something much more important than kneeling down in my room for morning prayers. The Mass was given to us by Christ himself and it is an official, public and social prayer of the Catholic Church. When I kneel for

Color Ebony by Helen Caldwell Day, Sheed and Ward, 1951.

other prayers, they are merely mine. When I assist at Mass, I am united to more than 650,000,000 other Catholics throughout the world.

The priest who celebrates Mass is not offering a private prayer. He is officially appointed and consecrated to act in the name of the community. The Mass, then, is an official prayer of the whole community, a sacrifice offered by all Catholics, and has definite social implications.

A POPE'S CHALLENGE TO THE WORLD

Pope Pius XII reminded the world in these words:

How can we claim to love the divine Redeemer if we hate those whom he has redeemed with his precious blood, so that he might make them members of his Mystical Body? For that reason the beloved disciple warns us: "If a man boasts of loving God, while he hates his own brother, he is a liar. He has seen his brother, and has no love for him; what love can he have for the God whom he has never seen? No, this is the divine command that has been given us: the man who loves God must be one who loves his brother as well."*

Religion is not something entirely personal. We are not living in a spiritual vacuum. The teachings of the Mystical Body of Christ, the dignity of human nature — all human nature — and the brotherhood of man under the Fatherhood of God are truths which must be taken into account.

As we join with the priest in one of the three essentials of the Mass, the Offertory, we recall that the offering of the bread and wine is a symbol of our own offering to Christ. Can we put aside his almost stern reminder: "If you bring your gift to the altar and there recall that your brother has anything against you, leave your gift at the altar, go first to be reconciled with your brother, and then come and offer your gift" (Mt. 5:23-24).

In light of those words, what about the "Sunday Catholic" who is guilty of violations of social justice during the six other days of the week? Can he in good conscience shut the door on his actions during the week and come on Sunday to offer his gift, his Mass with the priest at the altar?

As the priest holds aloft the chalice, offering to God the wine soon to become the blood of Christ, he and all present pray: "We have this wine to offer." Notice that the words are not "I offer" but "we offer." It is the offering of all those present. Perhaps we are joined in this part of the Mass with a Jewish convert on the other side of the church; the young black

*The Mystical Body of Christ by Pope Pius XII.

college student attending Mass before his exams that day; the little old Italian woman who attends daily Mass; the Mexican family that recently moved into our parish; with the Chinese who is a professor at the nearby university. "We offer." Do you mean that, or are you putting limits on the "we?" Are you coming to Mass filled with bigotry, prejudice, ideas of superiority and of "keeping those people in their places?" If so, then your Catholic life is a lie.

The heart and center of the Mass is the point at which, through the heaven-shaking words of the priest, "This is my Body," "This is the chalice of my Blood," Christ's own body and blood become present upon the altar. The Consecration is the climax of the Mass. It is a renewal of Calvary. On Calvary, Christ's blood was poured out to win the grace of salvation for every human soul. In the Mass, the merits won at the price of that blood are channeled to mankind. And the Catholic Church will not have us forget that no one is excluded from the merits of that blood. Pope Pius XII, seeing the need of reminding the world, particularly Catholics, of this fundamental truth, spoke out in unmistakable words:

> Men may be separated by nationality and race, but our Savior poured out his blood to reconcile all men to God through the cross, and bid them all unite in one body.*

ALL CHILDREN OF ONE FATHER

We can never become individualistic about the Mass. When we kneel before the altar to join with the priest at Mass, we must realize that we are all members of one family. Every Catholic shares in the fruits of every Mass. No matter how unknown or obscure a Catholic may be — were he to die forgotten by friends and relatives, Christ and the Church will not forget him. He shares in the same benefits from Masses offered on thousands of altars as do we. Perhaps the graces from a Mass we have heard will contribute to his salvation. Perhaps the fruits of some Mass at which a few African natives or Chinese peasants are present will be the means of helping us toward heaven.

As we glance upwards toward the body of Christ and the chalice of his blood raised aloft by the priest for our adoration, we cannot help but remember that his body was broken and his blood shed for everyone without exception. All Catholics — it matters not their race or nationality or

*The Mystical Body of Christ by Pope Pius XII.

shade of skin — are united in a large family of brothers and sisters with Christ present on the altar as the Head of that family.

"The parish," remarked Pope Pius XI on one occasion, "is a family in which the parish church is the home and the altar the hearth from which Jesus Christ gives food to its members along with all his graces and blessings."

Shortly after the Consecration, the priest and people recite the Our Father. Christ himself taught the world this prayer, and so it is fitting that it should find a place in the Mass. Without going any further than the opening phrase, the twentieth century world can learn an important lesson. Every race and every nation — Europeans or Asiatics or Americans, black or yellow or white, Jews or Ayrans — all have an equal right to say, "Our Father, who art in heaven." If Christ himself has reminded us of this right, and indeed commanded all equally to recite this prayer, then what power on earth has a right to reject the implications of those words?

Some time ago a full-page advertisement appeared in a national magazine. It was exceptionally striking, for it was not a plea to buy anything or to take a vacation cruise. The page was headed, in bold type, by the simple phrase: "America On Its Knees." Below this was a large, colored picture of Uncle Sam in his red, white and blue suit, kneeling in prayer, hands earnestly clasped, eyes gazing upwards. Beside the kneeling figure were these words:

> America on its knees. . . . not beaten there by hammer and sickle, but freely, intelligently, responsibly, confidently, powerfully. . . . We need fear nothing or no one . . . except God. . . . Our Father in heaven: we pray that you save us from ourselves. The world that you have made for us to live in peacefully, we have made into an armed camp. . . . We have turned from you to go our own selfish way. . . . Inspire us with wisdom, all of us of every color and race. . . . To use our wealth and strength to help our brother, instead of destroying him. . . .

The eyes of the world are on America — on the place of that one man in ten in America. Newspapers in India have headlined racist incidents. Radios in Moscow proclaim the unchristian ills suffered by minority groups in America. Sometimes the tables have been turned, and minority groups have terrorized the majority.

Everyone who professes to live under the name "Christian" — and certainly one who lives the tenets of Catholicism — has the source of inspiration and strength, plus the impelling motive to help his brother.

In the last analysis, the solution to this problem is a spiritual one — putting Christ's principles to work.

The Catholic who receives Holy Communion on Saturday night or Sunday and maintains an attitude of discrimination the rest of the week is living a contradiction, a sham Catholicity. If we follow the life of Christ, we will notice that the two things which excited his just anger were duplicity and hypocrisy. It is bad enough for modern pagans to reject the doctrines of the universal Fatherhood of God, the brotherhood of man and the Mystical Body of Christ, but it is infinitely worse for modern Christians who, while proclaiming belief in these truths, reject them in their daily lives. "Woe to. . . . you frauds!"

The social implications of the liturgy of the Catholic Church are not founded on *pity* for the common man. They are founded on *reverence* for him.

This, then, is not a plea for pity or sentiment. It is a prayer that the world may once more recognize the sublime dignity of human nature — all human nature.

The Catholic Church reminds us that she is the champion and defender of men, not because their state is at times so miserable, but because human nature is at all times so sublime.

WHY PREJUDICE MAKES NO SENSE

Prejudice (whether on the part of the majority against minorities or on the part of minority groups against the majority) is rooted in emotionalism. Its solution for a person of good will is founded upon reason and basic moral principles. Here is an outline developing this fact.

I — The unity of all men.

    A — Natural unity.

        1 — The soul of every man has the same spiritual origin; God created every human being.

        2 — The body of every man has the same physical origin: our first parents.

        3 — God has given all men a common dwelling place with natural rights to share its resources.

        4 — All men are interdependent economically and in society.

    B — Supernatural unity.

        1 — All men have the same supernatural destiny, heaven. That is why each and every individual was created by God.

2 — Christ died to redeem all men. As Catholics are reminded at Mass: "This is the cup of my blood, the blood of the new and everlasting covenant. It will be shed for you and for all men."

3 — All men are united in a common bond of love with God. "How can we claim to love the divine Redeemer, if we hate those whom he has redeemed?" (Pope Pius XII, *The Mystical Body of Christ.*)

4 — All men are called to a spirit of unity and fraternal charity in the Church established by Jesus Christ.

a — "There is but one body and one Spirit. . . . There is one Lord, one faith, one baptism; one God and Father of all" (Eph. 4:4-5).

b — "If you bring your gift to the altar and there recall that your brother has anything against you, leave your gift at the altar, go first to be reconciled with your brother, then come and offer your gift" (Mt. 5:23-24).

c — The doctrine of the Mystical Body of Christ: "The body is one and has many members, but all the members, many though they are, are one body. . . . There are, indeed, many different members, but one body. The eye cannot say to the hand, 'I do not need you.' . . . Even those members of the body which seem less important are in fact indispensable. . . . God has so constructed the body as to give greater honor to the lowly members, that there may be no dissension in the body, but that all the members may be concerned for one another. If one member suffers, all the members suffer with it; if one member is honored, all the members share its joy. You, then, are the body of Christ. Every one of you is a member of it" (I Cor. 12:12; 20-27).

II — The natural equality of all men.

A — Founded upon the very nature of man.

1 — All men have been endowed by their creator with the same essential faculties of intellect and free will.

2 — Human rights spring from human nature; they are not conferred by other men. "Since all men possess a rational soul and are created in God's likeness, since they have the same nature and origin, have been redeemed

by Christ, and enjoy the same divine calling and destiny, the basic equality of all must receive increasingly greater recognition" (Vatican II, *Pastoral Constitution on the Church in the Modern World,* No. 29).

B — The right to human life (which implies other rights to carry on life as a human being: the right to work, to obtain a reasonable livelihood, to education, decent housing, to esteem and honor, to worship God).

1 — One cannot own anything until he is already alive. Life is a prerequisite of ownership. Therefore, no man owns even his own life. The owner of human life is not man but God, who gave life to man.

2 — Interference with life, or denial of rights inherent in carrying on human life, is not within the province of another human being.

III —Relative to prejudice giving rise to acts of discimination, hatred or the demeaning of an individual, legal, sociological or good-will considerations are secondary. Basic to the problem is the fact that the law of God and the natural law are flaunted, for which violators will one day answer to God. "True, all men are not alike from the point of view of varying physical power and the diversity of intellectual and moral resources. Nevertheless, with respect to the fundamental rights of the person, every type of discrimination, whether social or cultural, whether based on sex, race, color, social condition, language, or religion, is to be overcome and eradicated as contrary to God's intent" (Vatican II, *Pastoral Constitution on the Church in the Modern World,* No. 29).

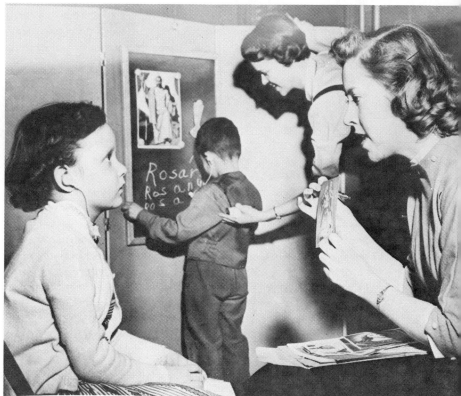

*Every layman,
by virtue of the very gifts
bestowed upon him,
is at the same time a witness
and a living instrument of the
mission of the Church herself.*
— Vatican Council II, *Dogmatic
Constitution on the Church,* 33.

CHAPTER 13

The Meaning of Christian Stewardship

Give me an account of your service. — *Luke 16:2*

Every Catholic has rights and duties. As for his rights, he has a special claim to the means of grace supplied by the Church. In turn, he has the duty to obey his ecclesiastical superiors in spiritual matters, and he also has the duty of working with them in God's service. This latter duty, to work in God's service, is a very broad obligation. Some people think that they have done their share by giving money, but that might be the least of all the things they could do. In many cases, God may want their talents much more than their money. When a swimmer is drowning, a donation to the lifeguard's fund just will not do him much good.

In recent years, a particular term has been stressed to indicate our duty of working with the Church to help others: stewardship. We can define Christian stewardship as the *individual's responsibility to manage his life and property with proper regard for the needs of others.*

It was at a busy intersection with a line of cars waiting for a traffic light. One motorist's car stalled. Anxiously he got out, lifted up the hood and began to try to solve the problem as quickly as possible. The driver behind him began honking his horn impatiently. Finally the motorist in trouble went over to the restless motorist leaning on his horn and said quietly: "I tell you what. If you will fix my car I'll be glad to keep blowing your horn."

Many "Christians," seeing others in need of help, seeing society in need of being "Christianized," stand by and honk instead of helping. To put it another way: the sense of stewardship has been largely lost in today's society.

Saint Paul gave a stark reminder of the "esprit de corps" that Christians should have when he said, "You are strangers and aliens no longer" (Eph. 2:19). In certain languages the word for "stranger" and the word for "enemy" is the same. Among the Greeks and Romans the stranger was looked upon as a barbarian and an enemy. In English the word stranger originally meant foreigner, one who does not belong. There is an implication of a gap between people. Stewardship is the catalyst which can narrow such a gap.

Stewardship is based upon love — of God and neighbor — and implies service. Three words sum it up, and have an intimate relationship, and interact with each other: *Know, Love, Serve.*

Our life is not entirely our own. It has been entrusted to us by God and is the instrument by which we are to work out our own salvation and the instrument by which we are to help others. The Christian is to be *in* the world, but not *of* the world. The Vatican Council spoke repeatedly of self-renewal, knowing that if enough people truly renew themselves, they will begin to renew the face of the earth. Stewardship, the voluntary and proportionate sharing of time, ability and material resources, when rightly motivated is a true act of worship of God.

CHRIST AND STEWARDSHIP

Read the teaching of Christ in the New Testament. There is scarcely a duty which is referred to implicitly or explicitly more often than stewardship. Christ used parables to teach. Most of the parables make the following three points: Regarding all things that man possesses, man did not bring them into existence, they are gifts of God; we must not use them selfishly, but rather for the glory of God and the good of our fellow man; we must be prepared by their proper use to give an account of our stewardship of these possessions.

Apply these thoughts to the parables of Christ:
The sower and the seed (Mt. 13:4ff).
The good Samaritan (Lk. 10:30ff).
The rich man and the beggar (Lk. 16:19ff).
The ten virgins (Mt. 25:1ff).
In particular, recall the parable of the silver pieces:

The case of a man who was going on a journey is similar. He called in his servants and handed his funds over to them according to each man's abilities. To one he disbursed five thousand silver pieces, to a second two thousand, and to a third a thousand. Then he went away. Immediately the man who received the five thousand went to invest it and made another five. In the same way, the man who received the two thousand doubled his figure. The man who received the thousand went off instead and dug a hole in the ground, where he buried his master's money. After a long absence, the master of those servants came home and settled accounts with them. The man who had received the five thousand came forward bringing the additional five. "My lord," he said, "you let me have five thousand. See, I have made five thousand more." His master said to him, "Well done! You are an industrious and reliable servant. Since you were dependable in a small matter I will put you in charge of larger affairs. Come, share your master's joy!" The man who had received the two thousand then stepped forward. "My lord," he said, "you entrusted me with two thousand and I have made two thousand more." His master said to him, "Cleverly done! You too are an industrious and reliable servant. Since you were dependable in a small matter I will put you in charge of larger affairs. Come, share your master's joy!"

Finally the man who had received the thousand stepped forward. "My lord," he said, "I knew you were a hard man. You reap where you did not sow and gather where you did not scatter, so out of fear I went off and buried your thousand silver pieces in the ground. Here is your money back." His master exclaimed: "You worthless, lazy lout! You know I reap where I did not sow and gather where I did not scatter. All the more reason to deposit my money with the bankers, so that on my return I could have it back with interest. You, there! Take the thousand away from him and give it to the man with the ten thousand. Those who have, will get more until they grow rich, while those who have not, will lose even the little they have. Throw this worthless servant into the darkness outside, where he can wail and grind his teeth" (Mt. 25:14-30).

STEWARDSHIP IN TODAY'S WORLD

When we speak of man in any generation, we must recognize him for what he is, and one of the most obvious of his qualities is that he is dependent. The poet Francis Thompson tells us that "we are born in another's pain, and we perish in our own," which is only to say that even for life itself we are in debt to others. We need our fellow men for companionship, for love, for sociability, for our education, for all the amenities that contribute to what we call living. "No man is an island . . ." is a phrase that has become part of our literature because it represents a fact that is basic to a proper understanding of man.

But as each man has a relationship of dependence with his fellow man, so too does he relate to the source of all life, the God of creation. For all that he is, and for all that he has, he must thank a wise and generous God and acknowledge a dependence on God's creative power and on his grace and goodness. This is usually done — we might even say instinctively done — in prayer, which recognizes the Lord's dominion over us and expresses our grateful thoughts for his enduring and loving Providence.

Both of these relationships of dependence — with God and with our fellow man — tell us something immensely significant about ourselves. They remind us that our lives reach out in two directions — vertically (as we may say) to the Creator, and horizontally to our fellow men. These facts must be expressed in our lives if we are to be genuine and not phony. To describe this human situation, the word used is "stewardship." It is, of course, an old word, and we remember it best in the earlier translations of the sacred writings of the Bible. A steward is one who is in charge of things which in reality belong to another. He is responsible for them and for their good management. What we must remember about man is that, for the years of his life, he is steward of all that has been given him — all that is his of time, ability, of opportunity, of special talent, and of material goods. They are held by him for his use, and he is responsible for their good management — not certainly as their creator, not even as their owner, but precisely as their steward. This is a fact of life that should speak volumes for all of us.

WHAT CAN WE SHARE?

Most immediately of all, stewardship suggests that what we have in excess of what we need must be shared with those in want. What is it that we can share with others? There is, first of all and best of all, ourselves. We can share our happiness and joy, and we can share our fun and laughter; we can share our love and our affections, we can share our strength and our vitality. To those whose lives lack all or some of these elements, there are no greater gifts to give. We can share a gift of song, a sense of beauty, a kindly phrase, a helping hand, a warm heart. All of these should be part of every man's living experience, and where they are absent we must make them present. Each one in a special way can give of talent and ability, even when these appear to be of a humble sort. It is not the size of the gift that counts, it is the willingness of the giver. We must share with others not just in proportion to what we have, but rather in proportion to the other's need. To promote this human situation is to promote human development and generate peace among men and nations.

We must of course apply the rule of stewardship to our possessions as well as to ourselves. We are required to share an abundance that may be ours with those less fortunate. Unhappily, the temptation too often is to make some necessary donation and avoid as much as possible any real involvement. The more precious thing to give is ourselves, and if this is held back our stewardship is incomplete.

The Vatican Council sums up the concept of stewardship in these words: "Laymen are not only bound to penetrate the world with a Christian spirit. They are also called to be witnesses to Christ in all things in the midst of human society" *(Pastoral Constitution on the Church in the Modern World, No. 43)*.

CHURCH SUPPORT AND VIRTUE

How guilty is the priest of God if he does not preach virtue to the people of God! The priest must preach virtue: the virtue of penance, with strong reminders about Confession, or the virtue of religion, with strong reminders about attending Mass or receiving Holy Communion.

The financial support of the church involves two virtues, the virtue of justice and the virtue of generosity. May the priest fail to remind the people of the virtues of justice and generosity as they apply to the support of the church? May the priest hesitate to talk straight talk about parish financing because it is a delicate subject and must be handled carefully? May the priest allow the parish to deteriorate, or the educational mission of the parish to slip because he might unwittingly and unintentionally offend? In short the pastor of souls *must* talk about money in parish life.

Church support involves the virtue of justice. Now justice deals with debts. The weekly collection involves justice because we owe God a debt. Justice is a precise virtue. We do not pay the cashier at the supermarket some vague amount, we pay exactly. We do not owe God a vague amount. We must try to be precise about the amount owed in support of the parish. This precise amount is based on the needs of the parish, the needs of the Church throughout the world, and our own income.

Justice is not an appealing virtue when we are the debtor, the one who owes. Justice is unpopular to the debtor because it seems to squeeze him. Justice can be an unpopular virtue because the parishioner is the debtor to

God, and a priest does not usually discuss the justice involved in church support.

Generosity is a more appealing and popular virtue. You are appealing to a person's noble sense when you ask him to be generous. The priest usually speaks of *generosity* in connection with the weekly offering. If $5.00 per Sunday is what you owe in justice, and you give $8.00, then the extra $3.00 represents your generosity. These amounts vary with the income of the parishioner and the general economy. These amounts have been selected to illustrate that you cannot be generous until you have been just.

All virtues are good habits. There is no virtue that is not a good habit. Habit is a fixed tendency which results from the same repeated acts. You are virtuous in regard to your parish when you make a habit of responding regularly, justly and generously.

Make your "church support" a good habit. Make your offering a regular part of your weekly budget. Prepare your offering ahead of time. Get in the habit of using your envelope regularly and your reward will be great.

THE WEEKLY PARISH OFFERING

Our weekly parish offering or collection, can be a cold and meaningless gesture, or it can be an event of beautiful significance among the religious acts of our lives.

For some, the weekly collection is a gesture devoid of meaning. . . . reach into the pocket, toss a coin, avoid being embarrassed by looking cheap in front of others. For some, the collection seems an undignified racket, ushers bustling, baskets passing, coins clanking, purses clicking, people shuffling. . . . all so earthy and materialistic against the backdrop of the Holy Mass going on up front.

But the Offertory collection exists at Mass because it fits at Mass. The collection is not a racket but an expression of faith. The Mass renews the death of Christ on the cross. As Christ offers his very life for us, the follower of Christ feels moved to offer something in return. We symbolically seal our relationship with him in his moment of offertory. The collection dramatizes our offertory.

In another way the collection fits into the scheme of our religious worship. As we pause to note that all we have is from God — our talents, our health, opportunity, freedom, faith — we are moved to give to him in return. The collection dramatizes our gratitude.

Sometimes we might choose to give money to God as an act of penance for our sins. Because I used the money to buy sin, or the instrument of sin, I now part from my money in atonement for sin. The collection could dramatize penance.

Sometimes we give money to God as a prayer of petition: "I give to you, O Lord. . . . please give to me. . . . or to my son. . . . or to my daughter. . . . or wife. . . . or husband. . . ." The collection dramatizes prayerful petition.

Therefore, the next time I reach into my pocket or purse for my offering, it will not be an empty gesture to avoid being embarrassed before men, but it will be a meaningful gesture so that God will not be ashamed of me. The collection will not seem a racket, but religion. The bustling ushers will be my messengers to God, the clanking of the coins will be the bell sounds of my gratitude, the clicking of purses will be the clatter of acclaim to our God, the people shuffling will be the stirring of community response to God's presence among us.

I cannot offer a trifle to God when he gave me everything. I am not very grateful if God gave me hundreds and I give him ones. I am not very penitent if my sin costs me fifty dollars and my atonement is fifty cents. I am not very strong in petitioning when I ask for a miracle and give a mite.

The weekly collection is a significant religious act. It is God challenging me to honest offertory, generous gratitude, sincere penance, and powerful petition.

YOU ARE GOD'S STEWARD

Stewardship implies the practical recognition that a man is not an exclusive master of his talents, energies and possessions. These are gifts of God and for their use we must answer to God. Not only money but skills, artistic abilities, mental acumen, education, the measure of grace, all must be used not only for our own salvation but for the spread of God's earthly kingdom on earth and shared with others for their temporal and eternal welfare. I am my brother's keeper. The beatitudes enunciated at the Sermon on the Mount were not "self-centered" but "other-centered."

In our times a special obligation binds us to make ourselves the neighbor of absolutely every person, and of actively helping him when he comes across our path, whether he be an old person abandoned by all, a foreign laborer unjustly looked down upon, a refugee, a child born of an unlawful union and wrongly suffering for a sin he did not commit, or a hungry person who disturbs our conscience by recalling the voice of the Lord: "As long as you did it for one of these, the least of my brethren, you did it for me" (Vatican II, *Pastoral Constitution on the Church in the Modern World,* No. 27).

The whole concept of man's existence on earth is that every individual is a steward, an administrator of all that he is and all that he has. To every individual talents have been given in trust, some more than others. "The first requirement," says Saint Paul, "of an administrator is that he prove trustworthy" (I Cor. 4:2). Loyalty and trustworthiness are indispensable in a steward, an administrator. The constant search for pleasure, amusement, for superficial materialistic realities leads individuals to neglect their life as administrators for Christ. And it is not just talk but action that the Master will look for. "What good is it to profess faith without practicing it?" (Jas. 2:14).

GIVE AN ACCOUNT OF YOURSTEWARDSHIP

As one
in public life
or business—

Are you serving the people justly and acting as a living example of Christian service? "It is our conviction that power, whether it be political or economic, must be conceived by the Christian in terms of service to his brothers" (Pope Paul VI, March 22, 1972).

As a
Christian—

Are you guilty of pride of race, or racial intolerance? "The only road to salvation is definitely to repudiate all inordinate pride of race or blood" (Pope Pius XII).

As an
able-bodied
citizen—

Are you conscious of and working toward the dignity of Senior Citizens? "Activities of the family apostolate . . . help for the aged" (Vatican II, *Decree on the Apostolate of the Laity,* No. 11).

As a
woman—

Are you serving the cause of the ideals of Christian womanhood? "Every woman has then, mark it well, the obligation in conscience . . . to go into action in a manner and way suitable to each, so as to hold back those currents which threaten the home, so as to oppose those doctrines which undermine its foundations, so as to prepare, organize and achieve its restoration" (Pope Pius XII).

As a
husband
or wife—

Are you truly faithful to and working toward the furtherance of the ideals of Christian marriage? "Christian families give priceless testimony to Christ before the world by remaining faithful to the Gospel and by providing a model of Christian marriage throughout their lives" (Vatican II, *Decree on the Apostolate of the Laity,* No. 11).

As a declared
follower of
Jesus Christ—

Are you doing anything to subdue atheistic Communism? "The remedy which must be applied to atheism is to be sought in a proper presentation of the Church's teaching" (Vatican II, *Pastoral Constitution on the Church in the Modern World,* No. 21).

As one who
has been given
talents by God—

Are you truthfully using them for God, the Church and your fellow man? "When much has been given a man, much will be required of him. More will be asked of a man to whom more has been entrusted" (Lk. 12:48).

As a
parishioner—

What are you doing in your parish? "There is no need to ask you to love your parish. That would be like asking you to love yourselves. You should never be content until you make of your parish a true model. . . . There you should live a truly Christian life, con-

As a
Catholic
layperson—

tinually manifested in love, prayer and esteem for sacrifice" (Pope Pius XII).

What are you doing for the Church and your fellow man? "For the exercise of this apostolate, the Holy Spirit . . . gives to the faithful special gifts. . . . From the reception of these charisms or gifts, including those which are less dramatic, there arise for each believer the right and duty to use them in the Church and in the world for the good of mankind and for the upbuilding of the Church" (Vatican II, *Decree on Apostolate of the Laity,* No. 3).

CHAPTER 14

Morality in Public Life

> The political community exists for the sake of the common good.
> . . . If the political community is not to be torn apart while every-
> one follows his own opinion, there must be an authority to direct
> the energies of all citizens toward the common good, not in a
> mechanical or despotic fashion, but by acting above all as a
> moral force. . . . The political community and public authority
> are founded on human nature and hence belong to the order
> designed by God. — Vatican II, *Constitution on the Church in
> the Modern World,* No. 74

Just after his last presidential election, Abraham Lincoln declared: "Being
only mortal, after all, I should have been a little mortified if I had been
beaten . . . but that sting would have been more than compensated by the
thought that the people had notified me that all my official responsibilities
were soon to be lifted off my back." A comment was made that Lincoln
should remember that in all his responsibilities, he was remembered daily
in prayer by many people, as no man had ever before been remembered.
Lincoln replied, "I have been a good deal helped by just that thought."
Then somberly the great president added, "I should be the most presump-
tuous blockhead upon this footstool, if for one day I thought that I could
discharge the duties which have come upon me since I came into this place,
without the aid and enlightenment of One who is stronger and wiser than
all others."

The famous Cardinal Cushing of Boston, on one occasion addressing
a large gathering of Catholic laymen in the city of Saint Louis, publicly
reminded our Catholic men and women of the United States of their particular responsibilities when he slowly and emphatically spoke these words:
"If all things are to be restored in Christ, the work will have to be done, in

*Let us have faith that right
makes might; and in that faith
let us to the end, dare to do
our duty as we understand it.*
— Abraham Lincoln, Address,
Cooper Union, N. Y.,
February 27, 1860.

photo by Paul J. Hayes

the main, by the laity. Upon our men and women, our boys and girls, chiefly depends the well-being of the Church and the state, of human society at large."

One thing that has unfortunately happened in our times, is that many Catholics fail to see the relationship between their Faith and their daily activity; between the principles of their religion and the way of life which is the source of their livelihood. This has become particularly true of many in public life, in government, in politics.

The principles we shall discuss will be applicable to those who actually hold public office; and also to any Catholic man or woman no matter what he does for a living, insofar as he is working for those who hold office, and can exercise a moral influence for the better; or in view of the fact that he votes at the polls on election day and must exercise this right in accordance with certain principles which we hear little about.

One young boy put this question to his father: "Dad, what does the expression 'practical Catholic' mean?" To which his father replied: "Son, that means that a man does not let his religion interfere with his life." Many Catholics in effect give that false interpretation to their life as a "practical Catholic."

PRINCIPLES FOR POLITICIANS

There are three major requisites to be found in a man holding or aspiring to a political office, and to be looked for and considered by those whose task it is to put people into political offices through the exercise of their right and fulfilling of their duty to vote.

The three qualities rendering a man suitable for public office are: required knowledge, moral integrity, and willingness to accept the office.

It is regrettable that so often today many candidates have only the third of these qualifications, and that so many voters utterly discount the first two.

The knowledge necessary for a public officeholder, and the knowledge which Catholics as citizens must demand of those whom they support, is easily available for any Catholic. He has the guidance of the encyclicals of the Popes, added to the clear principles enunciated by the Catholic Church on right and wrong. Any Catholic in public life who has not availed himself of this requisite knowledge on justice and rights, labor, Marxism, and the moral principles related to this specific job, is not worthy to hold office; and Catholic citizens may not in conscience vote for a candidate lacking this knowledge. If a friend of ours is in need of medical attention, we would not think of sending him to a man who is very willing to help but who never went to medical school. He would be utterly lacking in knowledge for the job at hand. Unfortunately we have no such training school for those in public office. We must leave it up to their conscience to obtain the required knowledge for their job, but we do have the moral obligation to refrain from voting for an incompetent candidate.

As for moral integrity, a Catholic has the ideals and norms of his Faith to guide him and the grace of the sacraments and the Mass to support him.

The absence of moral integrity in the lives of many in public life, both Catholic and non-Catholic, cannot be denied. There are those who falsely assert that there is hardly an honest Catholic politician. This is indeed completely untrue. There are countless Catholic officials whose activities are beyond reproach in private and public life.

Here is a challenge for those who have the first two qualities, the required knowledge and the moral integrity, to cultivate the third, willingness to accept public office. We cannot expect to improve the present lamentable situation unless we have many capable and honest statesmen in public office.

Here is a challenge for those engaged in political activities of any sort, though not holding an office, to support only men who are capable and whose practices are beyond reproach.

Here is a challenge to voters to seek out the best candidate and to renounce candidates who are incompetent, or whose principles are questionable to say the least. It is a challenge to those voters not to support a man simply because he is the candidate of a particular party, or because of the favors that might be gained.

Sufficient knowledge, competency, willingness to conscientiously accept and perform an office, honesty, moral integrity — these are the qualities we want to see in our public officials. These are the qualities the voters must in conscience look for.

THOU SHALT NOT TAKE GRAFT

When we speak of the seventh commandment, "Thou shalt not steal," Catholics often brush it aside lightly with the thought that stealing from anyone is about the last sin they would think of committing. But there is one violation of this commandment which we seem to have forgotten. That is the problem of graft and bribes and dishonesty in public life. Those are harsh words. And yet they must be applied to many socially acceptable practices in political circles. To banish these evils is the direct concern of those in public office and the indirect, but none-the-less very real, concern of all citizens and voters.

The unpalatable truth must be faced. Many Catholics are guilty of this practice so common in our day, in large ways and small, brazenly and openly or clandestinely and with a veneer of social acceptability.

Nor does it solve the problem to say that is the way things are, or that everybody is doing it, or that many non-Catholics are guilty as well. First of all, we have every right to expect more of Catholics, for they possess the Faith of Christ, they have at their fingertips the grace and strength of the sacraments, and the light of truth and the guidance of their Church. And secondly, right is still right no matter how many others are in the wrong.

Dishonesty in public life is at times used to gain a higher office or prestige but more often it is simply a means to obtain money.

Graft and bribery so widely accepted in political life may take many forms. All of them are violations of the seventh commandment and all render the violator, be he private or public official, be he Catholic or non-Catholic, guilty of sin before the throne of divine justice.

Sometimes an individual is rewarded with a soft job or a useless job, or is given an office just created for him in return for votes or for party loyalty, rather than because of a community or social need. To take a salary for such a job is nothing less than stealing.

The "spoils system" which dates back to the time of Andrew Jackson, and by which public offices are distributed to party supporters, may be allowed with certain definite qualifications. Only applicants who are worthy and capable, and who have the qualifications, may be appointed to an office. Certainly no office may be bestowed in return for a bribe. Any public official who rejects from a job a candidate who has the qualifications simply because he will not pay the required bribe, is thereby sinning. This sin is aggravated in the case where the individual appointed is not only less capable than another but is positively unworthy and incapable of perform-ing the duties of the office. In this case there is a double sin of injustice — against the worthy candidates and against the community.

No matter how widespread the evil, we cannot escape the fact that in the eyes of God it is sinful to demand payment in return for an appoint-ment to the police department, the fire department, any city or state or na-tional job no matter on how high or low a level.

When 200 applicants apply for an appointment to the police force, or clerical work at the City Hall, and an official makes it known that a certain amount of money will secure the appointment, that official is guilty of injustice and must restore any such money gained. To answer that the candidates are willing to pay for the job is no argument. A parent whose child is kidnapped is willing in the same way to pay, but that does not give the kidnapper a right to the money. Such a procedure of graft and bribery is essentially no different from robbery pure and simple.

Sometimes we hear the expression "honest graft." This phrase is a contradiction in terms. No matter how innocuous it appears, no matter how acceptable a practice of bribery is, it is still wrong.

The fire inspector who passes a building in return for a consideration, perhaps at Christmastime, or the police official who in return for regular payment closes his eyes to illegal activity or houses of prostitution, the building inspector who passes a building that should be condemned, the meat inspector who approves bad meat, all must one day answer to Christ their Judge.

The man who receives payment in return for secret official information; the man who pads the budget with fictitious expenses; the man who creates unnecessary jobs for his friends and supporters; the man who takes money in return for awarding a contract for public work; the man who sends men on the public payroll to work on his private home; the man who takes public property for his own use — every one of these is sinning against justice, and will one day face his Judge with an indictment to answer.

THE ART OF BEING HONEST

Thomas Jefferson summed up in a brief sentence his concept of the fundamental basis of good government. His words were these: "The whole of government consists in the art of being honest." Somehow or other, by a peculiar inconsistency in our day, a man who would not think of being anything but honorable, honest and upright in his private life, often feels quite free to engage in every form of corruption and graft in public life.

It is from two points of view that we consider certain prevelant abuses in this field in our day: first, the obligations in conscience from the viewpoint of a person holding some public office (whether it be a high position or the most insignificant one) or of a person working in the interests of a political party or an individual; second, the obligations arising on the part of voters to support only proper candidates and to oppose those who will not conscientiously and morally fulfill their public trust.

It is indeed at times difficult for a public official to be perfectly honest in carrying out his tasks. There are at present so many abuses that immoral conduct and dishonest tactics are taken for granted. Added to this is the fact that countless opportunities arise constantly in the daily life of a man in public office, with the realization that a little shrewdness will prevent detection.

Temptations are certainly present. And yet a sincere and honest man must be willing to go to all lengths, to make any sacrifice to preserve his moral integrity. And voters must be alert to see abuses no matter where they appear, and by all means denounce and reject dishonesty wherever it appears and in whomever it is detected.

Those in public office have an obligation in conscience before God to employ their authority for the good of society, city, state or nation, depending on their position, not for their own gain or advancement. To reverse this order would be a moral infraction and a sin. Thus a man holding an office and being paid with money from the public taxes, from the pockets of the taxpayers, who uses a large part of his time in working for next year's election, for shrewdly organizing his political machine, for buying the favor of others with his services, instead of using his time and energies for the job for which he was chosen, is guilty of a grave moral infraction.

In other ways too, sin can be involved in the exercise of a public office. Certain high officials such as governors have been known to grant pardons in return for favors; to use their office and even military forces to break strikes for a friendly employer; to bow to the unjust demands of some unions; to use the power of their veto in order to defeat legislation unfavorable to their friends or benefactors.

POLITICS AND THE EIGHTH COMMANDMENT

And today there is a widespread violation of the eighth commandment of God by slander and detraction during political campaigns particularly, but also between elections. There is no suspension of this commandment for politicians and those working for or with them. A person commits the sin of slander when by lying he injures the good name of another. A person commits the sin of detraction when, without a good reason, he makes known the hidden faults of another. Detraction does not cease to be detraction because uttered by a politician. Slander does not cease to be slander because it issues forth from the lips of a political constituent. And the obligation to repair the harm done is still on the conscience of a person violating this commandment be he a private individual or one holding public office.

The obligation of secrecy demanded by the eighth commandment is present not infrequently. Thus, a public official secretly knows that a piece of property will soon become very valuable because of a public building that will be erected in the vicinity. He transmits this information to a friend in order that he might purchase the property from the present owners for much less than he will soon be able to obtain for it himself. Here someone is done an injustice by the unlawful manifestation of an official secret.

There is the common moral infraction of the official who at his own whim and according to his own personal tastes distributes funds, benefits and jobs to his friends or to those who will make return to him in some way, often by a block of votes. Any official qualified to make appointments to public offices has a moral obligation before God to choose those who are most capable, most qualified and most deserving. To cast aside these considerations in favor of personal preference or personal gain, is sinful.

It is not easy for a sincere politician to conscientiously and morally fulfill his tasks. But it can be done. And it is a moral obligation incumbent upon Catholic politicians, Catholic voters and Catholic citizens to work to restore the Christian social teaching and the principles of Christ to modern society.

CHAPTER 15

The Atheistic Revolution

It is a violation of the will of God and of the sacred rights of the person and the family of nations, when force is brought to bear in any way in order to destroy or repress religion. — Vatican II, *Declaration on Religious Freedom*, No. 6

In 1818, in Trier, Germany, Karl Marx was born. This was one of the most world-shaking events in human history, for Marx was the founder of a philosophy which is the direct antithesis of Christianity. His highly successful movement has been popularly called "Communism," a rather loose term, and one susceptible of various meanings. It is more accurately called simply "Marxism."

A follower of Jesus Christ cannot, of course, subscribe to Marxism; but he can — and should — learn the principles of Marxism, in order that he will understand the realities of our times, and be able to apply the teachings of Christ to the problems that confront the world today. Moreover, whether we like it or not, we have much to learn in a practical way from Marx and his followers, because, as Christ pointed out, worldly-minded people take more initiative in their pursuits than religious people do (cf. Luke 16: 8).

The structure of what is known as the Communist Party changes from country to country and, taking a world-wide view, has changed through the years. We are not interested here in "the Communist Party" or the alleged differences between Peking and Moscow. Our interest here is rather Marxism-Leninism as a philosophy, as an ideology that has

*Regard all persons
without sentiment.*
— Lenin.

*You shall love your
neighbor as yourself.*
— Christ, (Mk. 12:31).

influenced the modern world, as an ideology which stands in contradiction to Christianity.

WHAT IS COMMUNISM?

It is impossible to define or explain the concept of Marxism or Communism in a paragraph or two. It is a system of thought and a way of life that seeks to dominate every aspect of the life of everyone.

Essentially communism implies a complete common ownership of all material goods and a denial of God. Communists hold that the world and all of its material goods came about without God, and so communism and all religion are diametrically opposed. Moreover, this is a way of life that will not be voluntarily accepted by individuals and nations but will be imposed upon the majority by the minority through violent means.

Whatever be the appealing form in which communists seek to present their doctrines, the following are some of the basic beliefs and aims of communism:

a. There is no God.
b. Everything is in motion; nothing is at rest.
c. Man is an animal.
d. Man is heading inevitably towards a classless society, the first step of which is socialism. This will be followed by a complete communist society.
e. This can be achieved only by violence, force, bloodshed and revolution. It is not possible to achieve the aims of communism by peaceful means.
f. The communist program and communist techniques are set up for the purpose of hastening this violent evolution, of hastening the advent of the classless socialistic society, the animal heaven of ideal materialistic human attainment.

THE KEY PERSONALITIES: KARL MARX

Karl Marx was born of a Jewish family in Trier, Germany, in 1818. His father decided to have all the family baptized Protestants, so Karl was baptized at the age of six. His father was quite well known as a German lawyer. At school Karl showed himself to be an intelligent child, and as he was growing up displayed a capacity for work that was to be a keynote of his life. He avoided the company of others. Very early in life he showed himself as proud and rebellious. Karl met and was attracted to a member of his own home town, Jenny von Westphalen. They did not marry for several years. He received the degree of doctor of philosophy in 1841. After his graduation Marx did not have a job nor did he seem interested in finding one, being more interested in atheism, socialism, and the reform of society. It was not until 1843 that the two were married.

Marx, through his study of atheistic philosophy, became an atheist and began to wage a war against religion. This was one aspect which was to become an important factor in all of communist philosophy. In 1849, with his family, Marx journeyed to England where he remained until his death in 1883.

Marx did not make very many friends. The most important by far was Frederick Engels, also a German, whom he first met in 1842. Engels became a close associate of Marx. During most of his life Marx never had a regular job, but depended on the generosity of others, particularly of Engels. It is ironic that the founder of communism was to a large extent supported and financed by a relatively wealthy man. And the key books on communism such as *Das Kapital* (Capital) were written in an atmosphere of poverty which really was the fault of Marx himself, since he had little desire to obtain any steady employment. There was seldom enough money even to live in frugal but respectable circumstances. When his daughter died before the age of one, there was not enough money for a funeral. Sometimes, Marx lacked sufficient clothes to go out of the house. When his wife was sick no doctor could be called because there was no money. Karl Marx continued his various writings in such circumstances and continued neglecting his family. It is remarked that on one occasion his mother said that Karl might better stop writing "Capital" and begin to make some.

Marx continually wrote and spoke with deep conviction about the plight of the working class and the supposed fact that wealth would constantly accumulate in the hands of a smaller number of people. The masses would become increasingly poverty stricken, and hence there is an inevitable conflict between the two classes. The Communist Party, in the mind of Marx, would be a guide for the workers who are uneducated and unfamiliar with the intricate theories of Marx. The workers need to be aroused in order to begin a revolution, and in this they need the Communist Party. The workers, when the occasion arose, would be prepared to use force and violence in their revolution.

The year 1848 is a most important year in the history of communism, for it was then that Karl Marx in collaboration with Frederick Engels produced the *Communist Manifesto* which contains many of the principal features of their thinking.

Karl Marx was not primarily an organizer or active revolutionary. He was a philosopher, a thinker, a writer formulating the theories of communism which others would put unto operation.

FREDERICK ENGELS

Karl Marx and Frederick Engels, as a team, were responsible for the original basic philosophy of communism. They were not primarily responsible for implementing the philosophy but rather of preparing the way and presenting this system of thought to the world. Although closely associated with Marx, Engels was of a quite different character and personality. Marx was morose and slow to make friends. Engels was of a happy disposition and a member of a family of wealth. He liked people and liked a good time. Like Marx, however, he was an atheist and a revolutionary.

Frederick Engels was born in 1820, in Germany. Engels spent much of his life in Manchester, England, to which his father's business took him. Marx lived in London. Engels was two years younger than Marx. It is said that he was a lover of horses and women. For twenty years he lived with one woman, Mary Burns, a worker in one of his father's factories, never having married her, and when she died took up life with her sister Elizabeth. It was not until she lay on her deathbed that he finally married her.

Marx lived in utter poverty, was of ill health, suffered from headaches and rheumatism. Engels lived rather well and constantly associated with people. It is in some ways strange that these two men should have been so drawn together and lived as intimate friends for forty years. Engels was a close collaborator with Marx. He had a brilliant mind, a fine memory, a knowledge of industry. Together with Marx, in 1848, Engels produced the *Communist Manifesto* and later was responsible for much of *Das Kapital*, particularly Volumes II and III. Frederick Engels died in London on August 5, 1895.

VLADIMIR LENIN

Vladimir Ilyich Ulyanov, who came to be known to the world as Lenin, was born in 1870, in Russia, of an upper middle-class family. Lenin's father was a school inspector with an earned title of nobility and a member of the Russian Orthodox Church. Vladimir was one of six children and a good student. As with Marx and Engels, atheism was the first step toward communism. As early as the age of sixteen Lenin drifted into atheism. It is said that about this time he violently tore a cross from his neck and threw it to the ground, spitting on it. When Lenin was seventeen his elder brother was hanged in Saint Petersburg, today known as Leningrad, along with four collaborators who were accused of conspiring in a plot to assassinate the czar of Russia.

In 1887 Lenin entered Kazan University and became associated with left-wing and revolutionary disorders among the students. These disorders went so far that Lenin was arrested. By the age of eighteen Lenin was reading Marx and organizing discussion groups. In 1891 he became a lawyer in Saint Petersburg. By the age of twenty-four Lenin had aged considerably. In many ways Lenin was a paradox. He liked some of the simpler things of life; he liked to play with children. He enjoyed life and people, loved the outdoors; was a practical joker. One great disappointment of his life was that he and his wife never had any children. But on the other hand he was deeply cynical and ruthless. He showed no mercy or tenderness, and as the years went on he had a singleness of purpose — violent revolution.

The conditions in Russia during the 1880's were characterized by discontent, and there were seeds of revolution gradually developing as a reaction against the harsh czarist regime. The writings of Karl Marx gradually filtered into Russia and *Das Kapital,* which had been written in German, was translated into Russian before any other language. This had the result of giving rise to several Marxist revolutionary groups.

By 1893 Lenin had joined an underground group in Saint Petersburg. In December, 1895, he was arrested, put into prison, and later exiled to Siberia. In 1900 he fled from Russia but did not by any means give up his ideas of revolution. Lenin, with his wife, lived as an exile in various parts of Europe, often under another name. They lived in second- or third-rate rooming houses in very poor parts of the cities. Following upon the thinking of Marx, Lenin grew in the thinking of revolution. He strongly felt that the reforming of the shortcomings of the social and economic systems of the day could not be accomplished by democratic means but must be accomplished by ruthless violence and the shedding of blood. These thoughts were inherent in the writings of Marx and Engels but were given a new impetus for action by Lenin.

In 1900, while Lenin was in exile, he published a left-wing revolutionary newspaper "Iskra," translated meaning "the spark." Although printed in Germany, it was smuggled into Russia and was read by the man who would later become known as Stalin.

In 1903 at a convention in Brussels, which was later transferred to London because the Belgian authorities demanded that the revolutionaries meeting there leave the city, Lenin entered into serious disputes with many of those present. Lenin strongly felt that a very restricted membership offered the only key to effective revolution. The others felt that a wider membership should be allowed. Lenin won and his group was called the "Bolsheviks," meaning the majority; his rivals who were in the minority were called the "Mensheviks."

While in England, Lenin made use of the British Museum for deep study, including a prolonged study of warfare and the methods of organizing armed revolutions. Lenin worked day in and day out for seventeen years until his time came in November, 1917. At this time revolution broke out in Russia. The German army defeated Russia, the czar's rule was in imminent danger of collapsing, and a left-wing regime headed by Alexander Kerensky took possession. Czar Nicholas II abdicated and the communist revolutionaries began to organize: Leon Trotsky, Joseph Stalin, Lenin. Through the famous November Revolution (which actually took place on October 25, 1917, and has become known as the November Revolution because of the difference in the Eastern and Western calendars; our date would be November 7, 1917), Lenin became dictator of Russia. From 1917 to 1924 a ruthless consolidation of power took place under Lenin.

Peasants' committees formed and included many of the poor as well as criminals. Lenin encouraged them to attack and murder the landlords, take their land for themselves. Lenin's orders along these lines often ended with the words: "Anyone who opposes this is to be shot without mercy."

Under Lenin a ruthless disregard for human life was common practice. There is a story that on one occasion a group of communist leaders were in conference with him. Lenin asked one, Dzerzhinski, how many traitors were then in prison, and was told that there were 1500. Lenin asked for the list so that he could see how many he knew previously as friends. Taking the list he put a cross on the top to indicate he had seen it. Dzerzhinski took the list and within forty-four hours all were executed and he so informed Lenin. Lenin was unmoved by the fact that a mere doodle on the sheet of paper containing 1500 names was mistaken for an order for execution and that 1500 men died on that account.

If a person had too much food or too many clothes, he might be considered as undesirable and either banished or killed. By the year 1921, men who posed a threat to Lenin were banished, but through these tactics a grave famine had arisen and much suffering resulted. Some have estimated that as many as five million people died. In March, 1921, some sailors of the Red navy in Kronstadt rebelled and some concessions had to be made by the Bolsheviks. In 1921 Lenin proclaimed the so-called NEP (New Economic Policy) in order to backtrack on some of the violent steps that he had taken.

In March, 1919, Lenin established the Third International or as it is otherwise known, the Communist International or the Comintern. This was the means by which Russian communism could branch out throughout the world, including the United States. The revolution and victory in Russia were only the beginning. The aim of the communists is and has always been the domination of the whole world. After a prolonged illness, Lenin died in January, 1924. His death resulted in a long-term struggle for power, which was to reach into our era.

The important contribution of Lenin to the cause of communism was the organization of and the active impetus given to the movement. Although he had a keen intelligence and was indeed a scholar, his more important contribution to world communism sprang from his organizational ability.

Marx, Engels, Lenin: From these beginnings, more than one third of the world has been captivated or captured.

CHAPTER 16

A 'Religion' That Changed the World

> The atheism which Marxism professes and promotes is a blindness which man and society will have to pay for in the end with the gravest consequences. . . . Class struggle raised to a system harms and impedes social peace and inevitably ends in violence and oppression, leading to the abolition of freedom. — Pope Paul VI, Address on the 75th Anniversary of the encyclical *Rerum Novarum,* May 22, 1966

A visitor to the Lenin Museum in Moscow some years ago noted the following statement under a picture of Lenin:

"First we will take Eastern Europe, then the masses of Asia, then we will encircle the United States, which will be the last bastion of capitalism. We will not have to attack. It will fall like an overripe fruit into our hands."

Whether Lenin actually spoke these exact words is academic today. The Marxist-Leninist philosophy and movement has in fact taken over Eastern Europe and the masses of Asia and is carrying out the encirclement of the United States. Hardly a month goes by that the news does not bring word to the knowledgeable observer that further inroads have been made in Europe, the Middle East, Africa, the far East or Latin America. For over fifty years this has truly been a philosophy, a "religion," a revolution on the move.

How is it possible that such a driving philosophy with basic moral

*Atheism is an integral
part of Marxism.*
— Lenin.

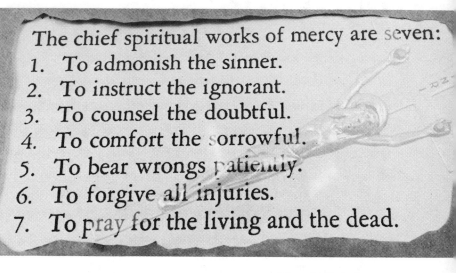

The chief spiritual works of mercy are seven:
1. To admonish the sinner.
2. To instruct the ignorant.
3. To counsel the doubtful.
4. To comfort the sorrowful.
5. To bear wrongs patiently.
6. To forgive all injuries.
7. To pray for the living and the dead.

*You shall do homage
to the Lord your God.*
— Christ, (Mt. 4:10).

and even humanitarian shortcomings and errors, can show such success through one generation after another? Years ago, Pope Pius XI, in his document *Atheistic Communism,* put his finger on one key to the answer, a truth which remains valid to our own day, when he said:

How is it possible that such a system — long since rejected scientifically and now proved erroneous by experience — how is it, we ask, that such a system could spread so rapidly in all parts of the world? The explanation lies in the fact that too few have been able to grasp the nature of communism. The majority instead succumb to its deception, skillfully concealed by the most extravagant promises (*Atheistic Communism,* No. 15).

The complete philosophy of Marxism-Leninism in all its fine details is most complicated and difficult to adequately appreciate. However, the fundamental goals and beliefs are not at all difficult to understand. Nor need we search far to find publicly stated these beliefs and the tactics to be used to achieve them.

The *Communist Manifesto* itself openly declares that the goal to be achieved is the forceful, violent overthrow of all governments and existing social systems, and complete world domination through communism. Says the *Communist Manifesto:* "They (communist revolutionaries) openly declare that their ends can be attained only by the forcible overthrow of all existing social conditions."

In addition to this fundamental goal of world domination, there is the basic theme of class struggle which will ultimately result in the triumph of communism. Says the *Communist Manifesto:* "Society as a whole is more and more splitting up into two great hostile camps, into two great classes directly facing each other: bourgeoisie and proletariat." And again: "The communists everywhere support every revolutionary movement against the existing social and political order of things."*

DIALECTICAL MATERIALISM

Marx and Lenin developed this fundamental communist doctrine by combining two concepts: first, everything in the universe is in a constant state of change as well as in a state of conflict — this is dialectics; second, there is no God and the world is composed only of matter — atheistic materialism. Picture a triangle. This represents motion. The left corner repre-

*Marx and Engels, *Basic Writings on Politics and Philosophy,* Garden City, New York: Doubleday & Company, Inc., 1959, p. 8.

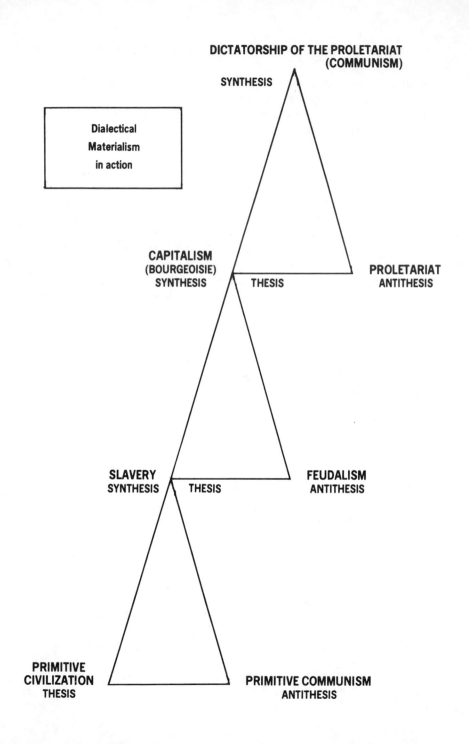

sents the status quo. The right corner represents the opposing force which inevitably rises to strike down the status quo. The uppermost corner represents the emergence of a third state resulting from the interaction of the two forces. This new status quo now becomes the left base of a new triangle and the entire process of violence begins all over.

The notion of dialectics implies that all forces are constantly in motion and indeed in conflict. A thesis in conflict with its antithesis results in a synthesis, which in turn becomes a thesis and another struggle evolves resulting in a new synthesis. Thus the exploiters (thesis) and the exploited (antithesis) through a struggle will emerge as an entirely new class: Capitalism emerged from feudalism; the bourgeoisie emerged from the feudal landlords; today the wage earners (workers, proletariat) (thesis) are in a struggle with the capitalists (bourgeoisie) (antithesis) and a new synthesis will emerge.

The dialectic, in the philosophy of Marx, is the logic or method of his theory of materialism. This is based upon a communist theory that ideas, social realities and nature contain within themselves their ideas.

WAR VIEWED AS NECESSARY

A key word in communist publications and propaganda is "peace." To those who know the philosophy of communism, war is vital to the accomplishment of their objectives. In the Marxist concept, preparation for war takes the form of building up military strength; in non-communist countries, it takes the form of open and secret apparatus waging a battle (often non-bloody) against non-communist elements. The basic philosophy to which every true Communist leader subscribes was laid down by Lenin: "Every peace program is a deception of the people and a piece of hypocrisy unless its principal object is to explain to the masses the need for a revolution" (General Committee Proposals submitted to Socialist Conference, April, 1916). What a far cry from the simple declaration of Christ: "Blest too the peacemakers; they shall be called sons of God" (Mt. 5:9).

To a dedicated communist, war is a means of carrying on politics. There are two types of war, just and unjust. Unjust wars are fostered by capitalists to further their own aims. Just wars are those of "national liberation." Just wars are those that promote the interests of the proletariat and help to defeat the capitalists. To the communist, then, a war is just and moral if it promotes the interests of communism; it is unjust and immoral if their interests are not furthered.

In the concept of Marx and Lenin, as well as those who follow in their footsteps, war is inevitable. It is necessary to bring about world-wide communism. Lenin categorically stated in a letter to American workers: "History demands that the greatest problems of humanity be solved by struggle and war."*

WORLD DOMINATION

Communist leaders down to the present day have not veered from the publicly proclaimed program of Lenin concerning the domination of the entire world.

Lenin in the year 1920 wrote: "If our international comrades now help us to organize a united army, no shortcomings will hinder us in the pursuit of our cause. And this cause is the world proletarian revolution, the cause of creating a world-wide Soviet Republic."**

Communist philosophy speaks of the inevitability of class warfare; the inevitability of the communist triumph. History has this in its plan and the communist program merely is hastening its fulfillment. This whole train of thought is what George Orwell referred to as "doublethink." "I predict the house will burn; then I pour gasoline over the stove. The house burns; my prediction is fulfilled."

Plans do not exclude violent overthrow of "capitalistic" countries, including the United States. Violent revolution will be cultivated if necessary. Quite often it has not been necessary because another formula has most often worked and continues to be utilized: "External encirclement plus internal corruption equals surrender." This is why moral corruption and general "demoralization" of any enemy is a goal to be worked for. This is why these elements are rooted out from Marxist countries and cultivated in others.

"Peaceful coexistence" is a myth. The clearly stated objective of communism is the ultimate domination of the rest of the world. Any temporary period of peace, any talk of peaceful coexistence or detente is only a tactic necessary for the moment.

ABOLITION OF PRIVATE PROPERTY

In the communist plan there is no such thing as a right to private

*J. Edgar Hoover, *Masters of Deceit,* New York: Pocket Books, Inc. 1958, p. 327.
**V. I. Lenin, *Selected Works,* New York: International Publishers, 1943, X, p. 199.

property. All things will be held in common. Each will be expected to work for the common good and each will receive necessities of life. "From each according to his ability; to each according to his need," sums up the communist attitude.

Relative to private property, the *Communist Manifesto* briefly gives their teaching: "The theory of the communists may be summed up in the single sentence: Abolition of private property."*

LAYING THE GROUNDWORK FOR REVOLUTION

Any non-communist government should be familiar with the ten clear steps proclaimed in the *Communist Manifesto* as the way to prepare a government for collapse and domination by communism. Any individual should know these steps so that he can fight against their accomplishment in his country. The following are the steps stated in the *Communist Manifesto* as desirable for achieving their ultimate objectives:

1. Abolition of property in land and application of all rents of land to public purposes.
2. A heavy progressive or graduated income tax.
3. Abolition of all right of inheritance.
4. Confiscation of the property of all emigrants and rebels.
5. Centralization of credit in the hands of the state, by means of a national bank with state capital and an exclusive monopoly.
6. Centralization of the means of communication and transport in the hands of the state.
7. Extension of factories and instruments of production owned by the state, the bringing into cultivation of wastelands, and the improvement of soil generally in accordance with a common plan.
8. Equal liability of all to labor. Establishment of industrial armies, especially for agriculture.
9. Combination of agriculture with manufacturing industries; gradual abolition of the distinction between town and country, by a more equable distribution of the population over the country.
10. Free education for all children in public schools.

*Marx and Engels, *Basic Writings on Politics and Philosophy,* Garden City, New York: Doubleday & Company, Inc. 1959, p. 21.

THE VANISHING FAMILY

Marx taught and true communists today believe in the abolition of marriage and the family. The *Communist Manifesto* declares:

On what foundation is the present family based? On capital, on private gain. In its completely developed form this family exists only among the bourgeoisie. But this state of things finds its complement in the practical absence of the family among the proletarians, and in public prostitution.

The bourgeois family will vanish as a matter of course when its complement vanishes, and both will vanish with the vanishing of capital. Do you charge us with wanting to stop the exploitation of children by their parents? To this crime we plead guilty.*

Engels considered the family a bourgeois relic. Through the 1920's and into the 1930's there were attempts to break down this institution. Abortion was widespread and would be taken care of for little or no money by the state; divorces could be obtained by postcard. Then in 1936 there was a complete reversal of all such policies which led to a breakdown of the family unit and what we would consider of the moral fibre of the country. The reversal was not brought about for moral considerations, of course, but Moscow saw what was happening to the country. There was a tightening up of moral standards for the national welfare.

THE VANISHING PATRIOT

In the communist scheme of things there is no such thing as the Christian virtue of patriotism. Devotion to one's country is to be abolished. Devotion to the cause of communism is the important thing. The *Communist Manifesto* puts it this way: "The workingmen have no country. We cannot take from them what they have not got. Since the proletariat must first of all acquire political supremacy, must rise to be the leading class of the nation, must constitute itself the nation, it is, so far, itself national, though not in the bourgeois sense of the word."**

LEGALIZED WOMEN

The substance of the communist attitude toward womanhood is stated in the *Communist Manifesto:* "What the communists might possibly be reproached with is that they desire to introduce, in substitution for a hypocritically concealed, an openly legalized community of women."***

*Ibid., p. 24.
**Ibid., p. 26.
***Ibid., p. 24.

DESTRUCTION OF THE STATE

The present plan and aim of communism is the destruction of the state as we now know it and the setting up of complete unquestioned dictatorship. Lenin spoke of this dictatorship as an iron rule, "quick and ruthless." The dictatorship of the proletariat, insisted Lenin, is won and maintained by violence against the bourgeoisie, and carried on with a power unrestricted by any laws.

Said Lenin: "The scientific concept 'dictatorship' means nothing more or less than unrestricted power, absolutely unimpeded by laws or regulations and resting directly upon force. This is the meaning of the concept 'dictatorship' and nothing else. Keep this well in mind."*

And again, Lenin declared: "The state is an organ or machine for the exercise of force by one class against another. As long as it is a machine for the exercise of force by the bourgeoisie against the proletariat, the only slogan for the proletariat must be to smash the state. But when the state becomes proletarian, when it becomes a machine for the exercise of force by the proletariat against the bourgeoisie, then we shall be fully and reservedly in favor of a strong state power and centralization."**

PUBLIC DECLARATION OF GOALS

Although at times individual tactics and statements may be confusing, the ultimate goals and the means to achieve them are not secret. At the very outset Karl Marx and Frederick Engels stated them and since that day communist leaders have reaffirmed the principles of Marx and Engels. Says the *Communist Manifesto:* "The communists disdain to conceal their views and aims. They openly declare that their ends can be attained only by the forcible overthrow of all existing social conditions. Let the ruling classes tremble at a communist revolution."***

*V. I. Lenin: *Selected Works,* New York: International Publishers, 1943, VII, pp. 123, 254.
**Ibid., p. 276.
***Marx and Engels, *Basic Writings on Politics and Philosophy,* Garden City, New York: Doubleday & Company, Inc., 1959, p. 41.

*Religion is the opiate
of the people.*
— Marx.

photo by Paul J. Hayes

*You shall love the Lord your
God with all your heart.*
— Christ, (Mk. 12:30).

CHAPTER 17

Marxism and Religion

> The Church has not and cannot adhere to social movements which, in finding their origins and strength in Marxism, have maintained its negative principles and the methods resulting from the incomplete and therefore false concept of man, of history and of the world, which is typical of radical Marxism. — Address of Pope Paul VI, May 22, 1966

The proclaimed objective of atheistic communism is the abolition of all religion. Lenin declared: "Atheism is a natural and inseparable portion of Marxism." Although this is the ultimate goal, because it is expedient for the moment, in some countries under communist domination, religion is allowed to continue or even is encouraged under the control of the communist rulers.

Marxism in proclaiming its hatred of religion has been at times very frank and public. Lenin declared in 1905: "Religion is a kind of spiritual intoxicant in which the slaves of capital drown their human shape and their claims to any decent human life." In spite of this, the movement, seeing the vast source of energy to be turned toward their own ends (for example, in propaganda for peace, appeals for pardons, etc.) has used religion and religious groups wherever possible.

COMMUNISM VS. CHRISTIANITY

Communism on the one hand and Christianity and democracy on the other are diametrically opposed, and this on the basis of several fundamental points:

1. Christianity teaches belief in God and the divinity of Jesus Christ; communism denies the existence of God and hates Christ.
2. Christianity and democracy teach the inherent importance of the

individual; communism denies the worth of an individual, teaching that he is only an instrument of the state in the class struggle.

3. Christianity and democracy teach the responsibility toward those in need — the corporal works of mercy; communism would exploit anyone to gain power and world domination. Its fine words concerning help of the workers are contradicted by its actions of ruthless oppression.

4. Christianity teaches that life has a meaning and purpose beyond the here and now; the materialistic teaching of communism teaches that our only goal is an earthly "paradise."

5. Christianity teaches the existence of a moral law which must be obeyed; communism teaches no such right and wrong except the norm of what will further its own interests.

6. Christianity, and in the last analysis democracy, teaches a doctrine based upon love; communism is based upon hate.

Communist leaders have declared that they follow the teaching of Lenin on religion and morality. Therefore, whatever their temporary attitude or actions may be, in the last analysis the attitude of communism remains the same as that declared by Lenin. The following are some of Lenin's clear doctrines and therefore the belief of any Marxist-Leninist today, whether in the East or the West and apart from any internal factions or power struggles:

We repudiate all morality derived from non-human and non-class concepts. We say that it is a deception, a fraud, a befogging of the mind of the workers and peasants in the interests of the landlords and capitalists.

We say that our morality is entirely subordinated to the interests of the class struggle of the proletariat. Our morality is derived from the interests of the class struggle of the proletariat.*

Communism has, from its inception, been the mortal enemy of the Catholic Church. Expressed in philosophical terms, communism refers to the Catholic Church in these words: "The Catholic Church fulfills the function of an apologist for exploitation."**

Expressed in practical terms, it has meant the murder and torture of countless thousands of bishops, priests, sisters, religious brothers and ministers as well as untold numbers of the Christian laity.

*cf. the pamphlet by V. I. Lenin entitled *"The Young Generation,"* published by the Little Lenin Library.
** *World Marxist Review,* March, 1960.

INFILTRATING THE CHURCHES

In spite of the fact that communism ultimately seeks to destroy religion and erase any belief in God, the churches are being used to suit its purposes for the present, and this for several reasons. The idea of using religion for their own purposes while in the long run seeking to abolish it, goes back to the *Communist Manifesto* itself:

Nothing is easier than to give Christian asceticism a socialist tinge. Has not Christianity declaimed against private property, against marriage, against the state? Has it not preached, in the place of these, charity and poverty, celibacy and mortification of the flesh, monastic life and Mother Church? Christian socialism is but the holy water with which the priest consecrates the heartburnings of the aristocrat.*

In addition, one who is at heart a communist and working for Red ideals, gains a veneer of respectability by being a good church member. Suspicions of him are cast aside; people will more readily listen to his opinions.

Churches, when properly infiltrated, can become a fine sounding board for the communist programs with labels such as "peace," "brotherhood," "justice for the workers," "cessation of nuclear tests," or "less military buildup."

Churches are an excellent means of reaching youth where at least the seed of Marxism can be planted.

If clergymen can be influenced, much has been gained. By deceit and in some cases by actual persuasion, clergymen can be influenced to support certain front organizations or some programs of the party. This gives strong support to their cause.

From several aspects the Church is an important target of communism: the teachings of the Church and those of communism are absolutely irreconcilable; the Church is one of the strongest enemies of communism; the Church properly infiltrated can be a powerful tool for furthering communist aims; experience has taught that lack of religious convictions in a man constitutes fertile soil for the seed of communism to grow in his heart.

Standing for all time as a symbol of the defense of Christianity against the onslaughts of communism is Cardinal Jozsef Mindszenty, who suffered torture, imprisonment and exile because of his religion. No one will ever be able to truly tabulate the countless thousands who have suffered and died

*Marx and Engels, *Basic Writings on Politics and Philosophy,* Garden City, New York: Doubleday & Company, Inc., 1959, p. 31.

in every corner of the world at the hands of Marxist-Leninists, under whatever name they were known in our modern world. The move to stamp out religion from the minds and hearts of men still goes on. And quietly, countless lives are the target of an atheistic philosophy which has changed the world.

PRAYER FOR THE CHURCH OF SILENCE

By Pope Pius XII

O Lord Jesus, King of Martyrs, comfort of the afflicted, support and consolation of all those who suffer for love of You and because of their loyalty to Your Spouse, Holy Mother the Church, in Your kindness hear our fervent prayers for our brothers of the "Church of Silence." Grant that they may never weaken in the struggle nor waver in the Faith. Rather may they experience the sweetness of the consolation You reserve for those souls whom You deign to call to be Your companions at the height of the cross.

To those who must bear torments and violence, hunger and toil, may You be the unshakable strength which supports them in their trials and fills them with the certainty of the rewards promised to those who persevere to the end.

To those who are subjected to moral constraints, often all the more dangerous because they are more deceitful, may You be the light which illuminates their understanding so that they may clearly perceive the straight road of truth. May You be the strength which supports their will, enabling them to overcome every crisis, every vacillation and weariness.

To those for whom it is impossible to profess their Faith openly, to practice the Christian life regularly, to receive the holy Sacraments frequently, to talk in a filial way with their spiritual guides, may You Yourself be the hidden altar, the invisible temple, superabundant grace and paternal voice, which helps them encourages them, heals their ailing spirits and gives them joy and peace.

May our fervent prayer be of help to them. May our fraternal solidarity make them feel that they are not alone. May their example be edifying for the whole Church, especially for us who think of them with so much affection.

Grant, O Lord, that the days of trial be shortened and that very soon — together with their converted oppressors — they may freely serve and adore You, who with the Father and the Holy Spirit live and reign forever and ever.   Amen.

CHAPTER 18

The Christian Response

Communism is intrinsically wrong, and no one who would save Christian civilization may collaborate with it in any undertaking whatsoever. — Pope Pius XI, *Atheistic Communism,* No. 58

Pope Piux XI, in his classic encyclical on atheistic communism, attributed the spread of communism to three things: failure "to grasp the nature of communism, a propaganda so truly diabolical that the world has perhaps never witnessed its like before," and "the conspiracy of silence on the part of a large section of the non-Catholic press of the world."

These three explanations, offered by the Holy Father in 1937, are just as true today. Even though decades have passed since Pius XI issued his condemnation of communism, and even though the communists have more than fulfilled the warnings of the Pope, still there are far too many people who fail to grasp the satanic nature of communism. So effective has its propaganda been that many are rushing to embrace their potential slave-masters. And the press of the world, as well as the media of radio and television, are conspicuously silent when it comes to exposing and criticizing the communist conspiracy.

It is no longer fashionable to be an anti-communist. People who were once quite concerned about the Red menace now would not even include it on a list of the ten most serious problems facing the world. Marxists have not changed their philosophy nor deviated one degree from their path to world domination, nor from their dedication to atheism and the elimination of religion.

The good of the
proletariat is the
test of morality.
— Lenin.

The chief corporal works of mercy are seven:
1. To feed the hungry.
2. To give drink to the thirsty.
3. To clothe the naked.
4. To visit the imprisoned.
5. To shelter the homeless.
6. To visit the sick.
7. To bury the dead.

If you wish
to enter into life,
keep the commandments.
— Christ, (Mt. 19:17).

We still have a moral obligation to oppose communism, an obligation that increases as the dimensions of the communist threat to the survival of our way of life increases. Carrying out this obligation will be difficult, but the Christian response to any moral problem in the modern world is difficult. Jesus never said that his followers would have an easy time in the world. He said that they would have their own crosses to carry, that they would be persecuted just as he was persecuted.

The important thing to remember, though, is that our Lord said: "Blest are those persecuted for holiness' sake; the reign of God is theirs. Blest are you when they insult you and persecute you and utter every kind of slander against you because of me. Be glad and rejoice, for your reward is great in heaven" (Mt. 5:10-12).

UNCHANGING GOALS

Through many years most Americans have refused to believe the often repeated objective of the communists stated by Lenin and his successors, that worldwide domination is their aim. Communist words from day to day proclaim peace; their actions indicate hostility. Moreover, by tradition Americans tend to trust in the good will or good intentions of others, but this attitude simply does not hold in our dealings with the communists.

Communist tactics involve reversal of positions at various times to suit their purposes, yet always aim at their final goals.

Marx and his successors proclaim that there must be a constant warfare between capitalists and wage earners. When the profits of one increase the wages of the other decrease. In point of fact, this essential part of the philosophy of communism has met an obstacle in practice in the United States. There are now almost as many stockholders as there are union members. Members of the proletariat are now part bourgeoisie! The class war becomes a war with oneself. Proletarian stockholders are undermining the philosophy of communism. Many years ago Pope Leo XIII, and subsequently his successors in the pontificate, urged that workers share in the ownership of the companies. As worker-ownership or profit-sharing in production and industry increases, communism will be further undermined.

Another argument against communism in practice is this: capitalism with all its shortcomings has been responsible for greater production, more equitable distribution of wealth, a greater personal freedom, than communism has ever been in spite of all its claims.

Furthermore, if communism produces such great benefits to individuals, and capitalism has such dire consequences, why is it that every year thousands upon thousands break family ties, and risk their lives to flee from communist-dominated countries?

One fundamental shortcoming of communism, of which the rest of the world should be reminded, is lack of respect for the individual. From the teachings of Marx and Engels to the current literature of the party, the individual does not find a place. It is always the class war, the revolution, the workers, the proletariat.

A second fundamental factor which truly represents an ultimately fateful shortcoming of communism is that it is based upon hate; Christianity is based upon love and so will ultimately triumph. Hatred is instilled in disciplined communists. The words of a once high official of the Communist Party on this subject are enlightening. Bella Dodd, after her return to Christianity, said:

> In the long ago I had been unable to hate anyone; I suffered desperately when anyone was mistreated. . . . Now, little by little, I had acquired a whole mass of people to hate; the groups and individuals who fought the Party. How it came about I cannot tell. All I know as I look back at that time is that my mind had responded to Marxist conditioning.*

CHRISTIANS HAVE BEEN INDIFFERENT

Communism is no mystery. There has never been a lack of knowledge of the communist plans. Their aims and the means to achieve those aims of world domination have been publicly stated by them. Yet, strangely enough, our opposition to those plans to dominate us has been half-hearted, sporadic; the communist threat has largely been met with indifference.

We are a peace-loving people and it is difficult to fully realize that communism is really based upon hatred, conflict, bloody revolution and suffering. In addition to this, the communists state their aims in jargon which has a very specific meaning to them but takes a little study for us to understand. Few have been willing to use the time and energy to do this.

Realization of the true nature and goals of communism, actively supporting effective means to combat it, and revitalizing the principles of Christianity in private and public life will bring about ultimate triumph.

The following quotations from key Marxist-Leninist sources give a

*Bella V. Dodd, *School of Darkness,* New York: P. J. Kenedy & Sons, 1957, p. 57.

terse presentation of the relationship between communism and Christianity. Here is what Lenin said about religion in general:

> Religion is the opium of the people — this dictum of Marx's is the cornerstone of the whole Marxist view on religion. Marxism has always regarded all modern religions and churches and all religious organizations as instruments of bourgeois reaction that serve to defend exploitation and to drug the working class.*

Frederick Engels made this statement, approved by Marx, on morality:

> We reject every attempt to impose on us any moral dogma whatsoever.**

Communist Directive 106, on how to destroy the Church, brings out the following points (published by the Congregation of the Propagation of the Faith):

1. Communists must enroll in schools conducted by the Church to act as spies while seemingly enjoying Catholic education.
2. Communists must be baptized, join the Legion of Mary and "use flattering phrases to allure the Catholics to themselves even by invoking their merciful God."
3. Communists must attend all religious services and "with flattering sweet talk spy on the priests."
4. The rule of spying must be: "Attract the enemy to destroy the enemy." They must find a prominent church member and provide him with all the facilities and the necessary documents to come over to communism.
5. Each comrade must understand that the Catholic Church must absolutely be ruined and destroyed.

WHAT YOU CAN DO

The following are some thoughts on what an individual Christian can do for Christ in the light of today's conditions.

1. *Study, work and be willing to sacrifice* for your convictions with as much dedication as communists devote to theirs.
   a. *Be willing to take on hard work.* Karl Marx used to divide his time between looking for enough money to keep going and doing

*Lenin, V. I., *Selected Works*, Vol XI, p. 664.
***Basic Writings on Politics and Philosophy*, Karl Marx and Frederick Engels, Garden City, New York: Doubleday & Co., 1959.

research at the library of the British Museum. He not uncommonly stayed there from 9 a.m. until it closed at 7 p.m. Then he would sit at his desk most of the night writing. "His brains resembled a warship which lies in the harbor under full steam, being ready at a moment's notice to set forth into any of the seas of thought."

b. *Be willing to practice self-denial.* Lenin, as a schoolboy, gave up skating to devote more time to study, because of the cause he believed in. His complete giving of self to the spread of communism from his earliest years added vigor and force in later life to directives like these to his followers:

"Learn and keep learning."

"Be ready to make any and all sacrifices."

"We must train people who will devote to the revolution not only their spare evenings but the whole of their lives."

c. *Seize every opportunity.* Leon Trotsky, one of the early communists, was sentenced to 18 months in prison. He employed his time learning four languages. Ironically he borrowed four translations of the Bible to do this.

d. *Develop a sense of cause.*

e. *Don't procrastinate.* "We can't postpone the revolution for one day," a communist official snapped back at a subordinate who proposed cutting the work-week down to five days. The sense of urgency is contributing much to the spread of communism. Be motivated by a consuming desire to bring the love and truth of Christ to all mankind, and no work or sacrifice will be too great for you.

2. *Help others* to understand communism's uncompromising objective: to dominate the whole world through a godless dictatorship under which the individual has no rights.

   a. Make it widely known that communism seeks to degrade and debase all human and spiritual values. Although they may withdraw from a position for tactical reasons, they never lose sight of their ultimate goal.

   b. The goal of communism was stated by Lenin: "It was Marx who taught that it is not enough for the proletariat simply to conquer state power in the sense that the old state apparatus passes into new hands, but that the proletariat must smash, break this apparatus and substitute a new one for it" (Lenin, *Selected Works,* Vol. X, p. 296).

   c. Lenin said frankly (and today's communists live by this): "In all countries where as a consequence of the prevalence of a state of siege or of emergency laws the communists are unable to carry on all their work legally, it is absolutely necessary to combine legal with illegal work" (Lenin, *Selected Works,* Vol. X, p. 202).

   d. Lenin said further: "Resort to all sorts of strategems, maneuvers and illegal methods" (Lenin, *Selected Works,* Vol. X, p. 93-94).

3. Insist that your *political representatives* acquire an understanding of communism and take enlightened action. Do not allow communist deception to go unchallenged.

   a. *Make your voice heard.* Letters should be sent to public officials requesting appropriate action.

   b. *Be fair.* Be objective and unemotional but firm.

   c. *Be alert.*

   d. *Avoid extremes.*

   e. *Be enlightened and not deceived.* Understand our meaning and their meaning of such terms as "peace," "democracy," "freedom." Be as resourceful for truth as others are for falsehood. "The worldly take more initiative than the other-worldly" (Lk. 16:8). "You must be clever as snakes and innocent as doves" (Mt. 10:16).

4. This is not a political but a *spiritual and moral problem.*

   a. *Do not neglect prayer.* Our Lady in her appearances at Fatima urged prayer and sacrifice, the recitation of the Rosary. The world will neglect this at its peril.

   b. *Any step however small, to restore religion, is a step in the right direction.* The number-one goal of the Marxists in any country is to weaken and eliminate any reminder that man derives his basic human rights from a personal God, not from the State. Since their number-one goal is to eliminate religion, it is basic common sense to restore what they would root out.

   c. *Keep first things first.* Be on guard against overlooking the primary spiritual values while seeking solutions for the social, racial and economic problems that beset mankind. Only when men recognize the spiritual worth of their fellow man do they show true reverence and respect for his human dignity.

d. *Deepen your own spiritual roots.* "Put on the armor of God so that you may be able to stand firm against the tactics of the devil. Our battle is not against human forces but against the principalities and powers, the rulers of this world of darkness. . . . You must put on the armor of God if you are to resist on the evil day" (Eph. 6:11-13).

e. *Warn the irreligious.* Those indifferent to religion are unwittingly fulfilling what the philosophy of Marxism-Leninism advocates. "He who is not with me is against me" (Mt. 12:30).

5. *Take a positive stand* and encourage others to do the same. Do more than just oppose Marxism.

a. *Restore what is missing.* Take constructive action to strengthen weaknesses and correct abuses wherever they are.

b. *Put love where it is missing.* One Marxist leader, Bukharin, recognized the dynamism of love that proves itself in action when he wrote: "Christian love, which applies to all, even to one's enemies, is the worst adversary of communism" (Pravda, March 30, 1934).

c. *Fulfill your responsibilities.* Vote intelligently. Take an active part in organizations to which you belong. Help raise the moral tone in public life and in the communications media.

d. *Stir up others.* Urge family, friends and associates to right wrongs they know exist in their neighborhood, community, and nation.

e. *Accent the positive.* Get better players on the team instead of focusing too much attention on those who, in your opinion, are fumbling the ball. Keep in mind the old axiom: "Push your own product. Don't talk too much about your competitor."

f. *Prove your love for the underprivileged.* Those living in poverty and misery, those who are objects of racial intolerance, are not impressed when Christians wait until there is a communist threat before coming to their assistance. They interpret this more as self-interest than as a desire to help Christ's poor.

g. *Overcome evil by good.* "Do not be conquered by evil but conquer evil with good" (Rom. 12:21).

h. *Take heart.* Communism must eventually fail because it is diametrically opposed to the nature of man. It has within itself the seeds of its own destruction. Rather than let down our guard, however, this fact should spur each one of us to take reasonable and effective steps to overcome communism.

6.   Bring back into every phase of life the *reverence for each person's divine worth*, which communists relentlessly strive to banish.

   a.   *Uphold the sublime truth* of the Declaration of Independence that "all men . . . are endowed by their Creator with certain inalienable rights," and that it is the purpose of government to protect the God-given rights of man.

   b.   *Restore elementary principles* to the mainstream of life:
   The existence of a personal God. Jesus Christ, true God and true man. The Ten Commandments.
   The sacred character of the individual. The sanctity of the lifelong marriage bond.
   The sanctity of the home as the basic unit of the whole human family.
   The human rights of every person as coming from God, not from the State. The right, based on human nature, to possess private property.
   Due respect for domestic, civil and religious authority.
   Judgment after death.

7.   Champion the rights of the *persecuted peoples*.

   a.   As Catholics, realize that there are fellow members of the Mystical Body of Christ who cannot practice their religion.

   b.   As a human individual, realize that there are fellow human beings deprived of their fundamental human rights and their freedom.

TWO POWERFUL MOVEMENTS

   Two powerful movements stand side by side in the world: Communism and Christianity. They stand diametrically opposed. Cardinal Mindszenty, speaking as a modern martyr at the hands of those who would root out his Church from the world, declared: "Persecution follows from the essential nature and internal organization of its ideology."*

   Much of the world is "communist." But much of that world must be contained behind iron and bamboo curtains, kept behind forbidding walls, prevented from escape by electrified barbed-wire. The philosophy has not "converted" one third of the world; force has. And the repercussions on the Church were presented to the world by Pope Paul VI:

*Mindszenty, Joszef Cardinal: *Memoirs,* New York: The Macmillan Publishing Co., Inc., 1974, p. 244.

There still is a Church obliged to live, rather survive, in the shadow of fear and in the asphyxiating and paralyzing darkness of an artificial and oppressing legality. It is a Church of silence, of patience, of agony because of its lack of the legitimate and natural right to profess, in perfect civic loyalty, its religious faith and carry out its mission of spiritual and moral education as well as its function of social charity.*

History, proximate or remote, will record the demise of the Marxist-Lenist movement known as communism. Christianity will preside at its burial. But perhaps more suffering, more martyrdom, more elimination of human freedom and dignity will yet be witnessed. For how long? The answer may depend on how many are now inspired to action and prayer.

Because communism is based upon hatred, is anti-Christ and anti-religion and is satanic in concept and execution, the weapons most efficacious in its death will be "the sword of the spirit, the word of God" (Eph. 6:17).

*General Audience, April 1, 1973.

CHAPTER 19

You Can Make a Difference

While the hierarchy has the role of teaching and authoritatively interpreting the moral laws and precepts . . . the laymen have the duty of using their own initiative and taking action. . . . They must try to infuse a Christian spirit into people's mental outlook and daily behavior, into the laws and structures of the civil community. . . . They must resolutely endeavor to breathe into them the spirit of the Gospel. — Pope Paul VI, *On the Development of Peoples,* March 26, 1967, No. 81

When one considers the problems confronting the individual, the family, and society, the temptation is great to want to go off to a deserted island somewhere. Or, like Pontius Pilate, to want to wash your hands of the whole mess. Or perhaps to wish that you had lived in earlier and more peaceful and less demanding times. While such thoughts may be temporarily soothing and distracting, we seldom have much time to indulge ourselves in them. The waves of reality soon come crashing down on our seashore of dreams and wash away our idle thoughts, leaving us once again surrounded by a tide of troubles.

There are two courses of action we can follow in this situation. We can bemoan our fate, complain that "everything always happens to me," and waste time and energy criticizing the present state of affairs. Or, recalling that the Cross is the symbol of Christian life, and drawing inspiration from the crucified Christ, we can meet the difficulties of the day head on, propose Christian solutions for them, and work to see that the solutions are properly and perseveringly put into effect.

As the Father has sent me,
so I send you.
— (Jn. 20:21)

photo by Edward J. Hayes

More than a century ago, Etienne de Grellet, a Quaker missionary, offered us these words of advice: "I expect to pass through this world but once; any good thing therefore that I can do, or any kindness that I can show to any fellow creature, let me do it now; let me not defer nor neglect it, for I shall not pass this way again."

WHAT CAN ONE PERSON DO?

Have you ever approached someone about dealing with some predicament involving your community? You explain the circumstances to him and he says: "I'd like to help, but I'm only one person, and what can one person do?" Often this is another way of saying, "I don't want to get involved." But if the person is sincere, you might be able to convince him that "one person" can do quite a lot, even in situations that appear to be hopeless. A few examples to prove our point:

One person, Saint Paul, despite floggings, shipwrecks, imprisonment, and frequent lack of food, drink, and clothing, preached the word of God throughout the hostile Roman Empire and caused thousands of people to reform their lives.

One person, Saint Athanasius, was a bulwark of resistance to the Arian heresy that threatened to overwhelm the Church in the third and fourth centuries. And how many people today have ever heard of Arius and his heresy?

One person, Saint Catherine of Siena, a young woman only in her twenties, helped to prevent war in Europe in the fourteenth century and later went to Avignon in France and persuaded the Pope to return to Rome.

One person, Joan of Arc, inspired the French people with her heroism in the fifteenth century.

One person, Juan Diego, a humble Mexican peasant, convinced the Bishop of Mexico City to build a church to Our Lady in the sixteenth century. Today the shrine of Our Lady of Guadalupe attracts millions of visitors and devout pilgrims every year.

One person, Bernadette of Lourdes, a French teenager, was the prime instrument in the founding of the world-famous shrine at Lourdes.

Now you might say that these people were different from the rest of us, that they were special, that they never had any doubt or hesitation about what they should do. But you would be wrong. They were human. They all had their moments when they wondered if it was all worth it.

Even our Lord, true man that he was, asked his Father in heaven to spare him the ordeal that was to come. But then, as his followers have done ever since, Jesus went on to do his Father's will, giving us a perfect example to follow.

We are to be God's instruments in the world. If you leave your garden completely up to God, it will be overrun with weeds. Why? Because God helps those who help themselves. It is not enough to wish that things would get better; we must work to make it happen. God gave us a backbone, not a wishbone. He has given us the intelligence to recognize what must be done, and he will give us the courage to do it if we ask him.

SOME EXAMPLES FROM AMERICAN HISTORY

American history is replete with incidents where the vote of one person had a major impact on the future of our nation. Thomas Jefferson and John Quincy Adams were elected to the Presidency by one vote in the electoral college. Statehood was granted to California, Idaho, Oregon, Texas, and Washington by one vote. President Andrew Johnson, who had been impeached by the House of Representatives, was acquitted in the Senate by one vote. The purchase of Alaska was approved by one vote. And the reason we speak English in America today is because a motion in the Continental Congress two centuries ago to make German the official language of the United States was defeated by one vote.

The next time someone asks what one person can do, or questions whether one person can make a difference, give him some examples and leave them with this thought: "I am only one, but I am one. I cannot do everything, but I can do something. And I will not fail to do that which I can do."

EVERYONE NEEDS OUR PRODUCT

There is a story of two shoe salesmen who were sent to Africa to probe the possibilities for markets on that continent. After a few weeks, two cables came back to the home office. One read, "Forget it. Four out of five wouldn't know a shoe if they saw it." The other said, "Send immediate reinforcements. Almost everyone needs our product."

Can we not say the same thing about Christianity? Christianity is what the world needs. What are you doing to bring this product to the world? We have all been put on this earth by God to make a difference. It does not have to be a difference that affects the future of the world, or the country, or even our own community. It might be just to provide love, understanding, and encouragement to members of our own family. It might be to show compassion and kindness to a friend or neighbor in trouble. It might be to defend the right to life of everyone from the unborn child to the senior citizen. It might be to work for racial justice, for a more equitable distribution of the world's goods to the less fortunate, or for the election of moral and upright persons to public office. It might be to press for the freedom of our persecuted brothers and sisters in communist countries. But whatever it is, someone ought to know that we have passed their way. Someone's life should be different for having come into contact with us.

To make a difference in this life will not be easy. No truly Christian life can ever be easy. Nor are we likely to receive the plaudits of the world for our efforts. We are called to be in the world but not of the world, a distinction that sometimes eludes us. Our reward is eternal, not temporal.

We are pilgrims on the road to heaven. We have certain responsibilities here and now but our destiny is the hereafter and forever. Christ and his Church give us the principles to follow in order to help solve the problems we face. We must put these principles into practice. We must do all that we can, individually and collectively, to exercise our Christian stewardship and to bring the true peace of Christ to families and society. We must let the light of Christ shine through us, not dimly but brightly, hoping to dispel the darkness of sin from the world in which we are travelers. We must proclaim by word and example the beatitudes and the other parts of Christ's blueprint for society which he spelled out for us in the Sermon on the Mount. And we must do so firmly and courageously, for we are members of the Church Militant, not the Church passive.

Having responded wholeheartedly to the Christian call to action, we can then say with Saint Paul: "I have fought the good fight, I have finished the race, I have kept the faith" (II Tm. 4:7).

The words spoken by General Douglas MacArthur in 1947 give pause for thought today:

"When at the time of the surrender I stated on the U.S.S. Missouri that the solution of the world's problems was a theological one, some people thought I was losing my mind. Today I hold to that statement more strongly than ever. Those who criticized me for it have shown that they don't believe either in democracy or Christianity. They have no faith. The world's problems are basically spiritual. Economics, power, politics, collectivism — these are but surface difficulties that come and go. Below these, and at the root of most of our troubles is a lack of religious faith and the sooner we realize this the sooner we will have peace and order."

EPILOGUE

Pope
Paul VI

This is a difficult time in the Church's life, yet it is also a time which God is blessing, a time rich in grace and full of hope. Today as yesterday, the Church is carrying out her mission of salvation throughout the world, and transmits the promises of redemption and everlasting life.

The Church today may be groaning, as St. Paul said of every creature, by reason of the pains of giving birth, which go before exultation at the appearance of new life; yet the Church also bears the Spirit of God within herself, the Creator Spirit, the Spirit of love and charity.

The spirit of division may be at work as usual in the Father's field and is sowing weeds there, but we were forewarned, and we will not allow ourselves to be taken in by its deceptions or discouraged by its intrusions.

The Lord's Spirit is also at work in his Church. He is not a spirit of contestation, but a spirit of renewal and peacefulness. He is uninterruptedly stirring up fresh undertakings, those of the apostolate and of holiness. He is launching us out into the deep, that is, toward the needs of the new age.

Let us meet these needs with love, with serious thought and, without giving in to the unwise tendencies of the secular world, without fearing the traps set by the Evil One, but being certain, as we are certain, of being in God's hands, of being carried along by his love.

Bibliography

The following is a list of some works used in the preparation of this volume and which the reader or teacher may find of use. The authors do not necessarily agree with the contents or approach of every reference book.

Anchell, Melvin, M.D., *A Second Look at Sex Education,* Santa Monica, California: Educulture, Inc., 1972.

Basic Teachings for Catholic Religious Education, Washington, D.C.: United States Catholic Conference, 1973.
Bird, Joseph and Lois, *Marriage Is for Grownups,* Garden City, New York: Image Books, 1971.
Bird, Joseph and Lois, *Power to the Parents,* Garden City: Doubleday and Company, 1972.

Catechism of Modern Man, Boston: St. Paul Editions, 1968.
Chambers, Whittaker, *Witness,* New York: Random House, Inc., 1952.
Ciszek, Walter J., S.J., *With God in Russia,* New York: Image Books, 1966.
Connell, Francis J., *Morals in Politics and Professions,* Westminster, Maryland: The Newman Press, 1951.
Connell, Francis J., and Weitzel, Eugene J., *Father Connell Answers Moral Questions,* Washington, D.C.: The Catholic University of America Press, 1959.
Connell, Francis J., and Weitzel, Eugene J., *More Answers to Today's Moral Problems,* Washington, D.C.: The Catholic University of America Press, 1964.
Conway, Bertrand L. (Rev.), *The Question Box,* New York: The Paulist Press, 1929.
Conway, J. D., *What the Church Teaches,* New York: Harper & Brothers, 1962.

Daughters of St. Paul, *The Catechism of Modern Man,* Boston: The Daughters of St. Paul, 1968.
Daughters of St. Paul, *The Church's Amazing Story,* St. Paul Editions, 1969.
Delespesse, Max, *The Church Community Leaven and Life-Style,* Notre Dame, Indiana: Ave Maria Press, 1973.
Derrick, Christopher, *The Moral and Social Teaching of the Church,*

New York: Hawthorne Books, Inc., 1964.

DeSmedt, Bishop Emile-Joseph, *Parent-Adolescent Dialogue,* Notre Dame, Indiana: Fides Publishers, Inc., 1967.

Documents of Vatican II, Walter M. Abbott, S.J., gen. ed., New York: Herder and Herder, 1966.

Fischer, George, *Generation of Opportunity,* New York: The Paulist Press, 1968.

Foster, William Z., *Toward Soviet America,* Balboa Island, Calif.: Elgin Publications, 1961.

Fox, Fr. Robert J., *Charity, Morality, Sex and Young People,* Huntington, Indiana: Our Sunday Visitor, Inc., 1975.

Fundamentals of Marxism-Leninism, A Manual; Moscow: Foreign Languages Publishing House, 1961.

General Catechetical Directory, Washington, D.C.: United States Catholic Conference, 1971.

Gibert, Henri, M.D., *Love in Marriage,* New York: Guild Press, 1964.

Gillis, James M., *This Our Day,* New York: The Paulist Press, 1949.

Hardon, John A., S.J., *Christianity in the Twentieth Century,* Garden City, New York: Image Books, 1972.

Haring, Bernard, C.SS.R., *The Law of Christ,* Westminster, Maryland: The Newman Press, 1963 2v.

Haring, Bernard, *Medical Ethics,* Notre Dame, Indiana: Fides Publishers, Inc., 1973.

Harlow, Ralph V., *The Growth of the United States,* Volume II, 1865-1943, New York: Henry Holt and Company, 1943.

Harney, Martin P., S.J., *The Catholic Church Through the Ages,* Boston: The Daughters of St. Paul, 19741

Hayes, E. J., and Hayes, P. J., *Communism Against the World,* St. Paul, Minnesota: Catechetical Guild Educational Society, 1962.

Hoover, J. Edgar, *A Study of Communism,* New York: Holt, Rinehart and Winston, Inc., 1962.

Hoover, J. Edgar, *Masters of Deceit,* New York: Henry Holt and Company, 1958.

Hughes, Philip, *A Popular History of the Catholic Church,* New York: The Macmillan Company, 1947.

Jacobsen, Marion Leach, *How to Keep Your Family Together and Still*

Have Fun, Grand Rapids, Michigan: Zondervan Publishing House, 1972.

Jeremias, Joachim, *The Parables of Jesus,* New York: Charles Scribner's Sons, 1972.

Kelly, Rev. George A., *The Catholic Marriage Manual,* New York: Random House, 1958.

Keraus, Patrick, *Sinful Social Structures,* New York: The Paulist Press, 1974.

Klewin, Thomas, *Love Thy Teenager,* Notre Dame, Indiana: Ave Maria Press, 1970.

Kubler-Ross, Elizabeth, M.D., *On Death and Dying,* New York: The Macmillan Company, 1969.

LaFarge, John, *No Postponement,* New York: Longmans, Green and Company, 1950.

LaFarge, John, *The Catholic Viewpoint on Race Relations,* Garden City, New York: Hanover House, 1956.

LaFarge, John, *The Race Question and the Negro,* New York: Longmans, Green and Company, 1943.

Lenin, V. I., *Collected Works,* Moscow: Foreign Languages Publishing House, 1961.

Levenson, Sam, *Everything But Money,* New York: Simon and Schuster, 1966.

Marx, Karl, *Capital,* New York: The Modern Library, c. 1906; revised and amplified according to the 4th German ed.

Marx, Karl, and Engels, Freidrich, *Basic Writings on Politics and Philosophy,* Garden City, New York: Doubleday and Company, Inc., 1959.

Marx, Paul, O.S.B., *The Death Peddlers: War on the Unborn,* Collegeville, Minnesota: Saint John's University Press, 1971.

Masse, Benjamin L., *The Catholic Mind Through Fifty Years,* New York: The America Press, 1952.

McFadden, Charles J., *The Philosophy of Communism,* New York: Benziger Brothers, Inc., 1939.

McIntyre, Marie, ed., *Parents You've Got a Lot to Give,* Notre Dame, Indiana: Ave Maria Press, 1972.

Mechanic, David, *Medical Sociology,* New York: The Free Press, 1968.

Miceli, Vincent P., S.J., *The Gods of Atheism,* New Rochelle, New York: Arlington House, 1971.

Mindszenty, Jozsef Cardinal, *Memoirs,* New York: Macmillan Publishing Company, Inc., 1974.

Norwen, Henri, and Goffrey, Walter, *Aging, the Fulfillment of Life,* Garden City, New York: Doubleday & Co., 1974.

O'Connell, Hugh J., *Stewardship: Call to a New Way of Life,* Liguori, Missouri: Liguorian Books, 1969.
O'Reilly, Sean, M.D., *In the Image of God,* Middleburg, Virginia: Notre Dame Institute Press, 1974.
O'Shea, Kevin, and Meehan, Noel, *A Human Apostolate,* Liguori Publications, 1972.
Overstreet, Harry and Bonaro, *What We Must Know About Communism,* New York: W. W. Norton & Company, Inc., 1958.

Papini, Giovanni, *Life of Christ,* New York: Harcourt, Brace and Company, 1923.
Paterson, Evelyn and J. Allen, ed., *For Women Only,* Wheaton, Illinois: Tyndale, 1974.
Pelton, Robert W., *One Hundred and One Things You Should Know About Marijuana,* Belmont, Massachusetts: Western Islands, 1972.

Rice, Charles E., *Authority and Rebellion,* Garden City, New York: Doubleday & Company, Inc., 1971.
Rice, Charles E., *The Vanishing Right to Live,* Garden City, New York: Doubleday & Company, 1969.
Robertson, Josephine, *Prayers for the Later Years,* New York: Abingdon Press, 1972.

Schwarz, Fred, *You Can Trust the Communists,* Englewood Cliffs, N.J.: Prentice-Hall, Inc., 1961.
Solzhenitsyn, Aleksandr I., *The Gulag Archipelago,* New York: Harper & Row, Publishers, Inc., 1974.

Tanquerey, A., *The Spiritual Life,* Tournai, Belgium: Desclee and Company, 1930.
The Tenth National Congress of the Communist Party of China, Peking: Foreign Languages Press, 1973.
To Teach As Jesus Did, Washington, D.C.: United States Catholic Conference, 1973.

Whitehead, K. D., *Respectable Killing: The New Abortion Imperative,* New Rochelle, New York: Catholics United for the Faith, Inc., 1972.

Wilhelm, Anthony, *Christ Among Us,* New York and Paramus: The Paulist Press, 1972.

Willke, Dr. and Mrs. J.C., *Handbook on Abortion,* Cincinnati, Ohio: Hiltz Publishing Company, 1973

Wolfe, Bertram D., *Three Who Made a Revolution,* Boston: Beacon Press, 1948.

Woods, Ralph L., *A Treasury of Catholic Thinking,* New York: Thomas Y. Crowell Company, 1953.

Wright, Cardinal John, *The Church: Hope of the World,* Kenosha, Wisconsin: Prow Books, 1972. Edited by Rev. Donald W. Wuerl.

Wurmbrand, Richard, *Tortured for Christ,* Glendale, California: Diane Books, 1969

Index